*Twayne's United States Authors Series*

EDITOR OF THIS VOLUME

Sylvia E. Bowman

*Indiana University*

# H. L. Mencken

## TUSAS 297

H. L. Mencken

# H. L. MENCKEN

## W. H. A. Williams

*Arizona State University*

## TWAYNE PUBLISHERS

A DIVISION OF G. K. HALL & CO., BOSTON

Library of Congress Cataloging in Publishing Data

Williams, W. H. A.
    H. L. Mencken.

    (Twayne's United States authors series ; TUSAS 297)
    Bibliography: p. 166–74
    Includes index.
    1. Mencken, Henry Louis, 1880–1956.    2. Authors,
American—20th century—Biography.
PS3525.E43Z9      818'.5'209      77-10800
ISBN 0-8057-7200-6

In Memory of my grandfather

Daniel Werner Hamm

# Contents

# About the Author

Born in Philadelphia in 1937, Dr. Williams attended various public schools in eastern Pennsylvania and graduated from Allentown High School in 1955. He immediately entered Lafayette College at Easton, Pennsylvania, graduating *cum laude* with honors in history in 1959. Receiving an Edward John Noble Fellowship, he commenced graduate studies in American history at The Johns Hopkins University. He took his Master's Degree from Hopkins in 1962 and his Ph.D. degree in 1972. Dr. Williams' doctoral thesis was a critical study of H. L. Mencken.

Dr. Williams began his teaching career in the History Department of Southern Illinois University at Carbondale in 1965. The following year he took up the position as the American historian in the Department of Modern History at University College, Dublin, Ireland. He taught in Ireland for six years, leaving there in 1972 to lecture in American Studies in the English Faculty at the Justis-Liebig University in Giessen, West Germany. He spent the academic year, 1974–1975, on a self-financed sabbatical in Ireland and the United Kingdom, researching a study on the social and cultural history of midwifery. He returned to the United States in 1975 to take up a position as a Visiting Assistant Professor in American Cultural History at Arizona State University at Tempe.

*H. L. Mencken* is Dr. Williams' first book. In addition to his writings on Mencken, he has published articles on midwifery, folklore and folk music. While in Ireland, he researched, wrote, and presented programs on folk music for Irish radio and television and he appeared frequently on Radio Eireann as a commentator on American affairs. He has also engaged in free lance journalism, having had material published in the Baltimore *Sun*, *The Christian Science Monitor*, *Opera News*, *Saturday Review*, and *The Progressive*, as well as in various Irish newspapers.

# Preface

What Henry Adams said of Theodore Roosevelt might also be said of H. L. Mencken: he was pure act. Mencken's accomplishments were not translated, however, into the acts of statecraft: he led no armies, built no canals, and never invited millions of voters to stand with him at Armageddon. Like "T. R.," however, "H. L. M." was a phenomenon. He was a force that went beyond any attempts to pen him within such easily defined catagories as journalist, literary critic, popular philosopher, social critic, philologist, editor, autobiographer, or satirist. Mencken was all of these things—and more.

However, trying to define that phenomenon, searching for the sum of all of those seemingly disparate yet somehow connected parts, can be a difficult and confusing task. For while Mencken transcended the limitations of compartmentalization, he did so without becoming the master of anything more than a highly idiosyncratic prose style. He was a good and very important literary critic but not a great one. As a commentator on American society, he was always observant and sometimes incisive, but he had no real theoretical or ideological approach to the subject. A pioneer in helping to introduce to Americans such European thinkers and writers as Friedrich Nietzsche and George Bernard Shaw, Mencken nevertheless saw ideas as gaudy banners to be waved instead of complex problems to be analyzed.

There may be a temptation, then, to lose patience with Mencken before the reader comes to know him. The reader may begin to want a different Mencken than the one he encounters—a better critic, a trained philologist, a genuine philosopher, a more consistant thinker. Mencken, the antispecialist, tends to displease most specialists in the various fields in which he sported.

Mencken's disinclination to respect the academic proprieties is one of the reasons for his continuing appeal. In an age of specialization, the man or woman who leaps the fences of disciplines is a kind of outlaw—a modern Till Eulenspiegel, an intellectual Robin Hood. There have been others who have carried out this role more elegantly and with much more impressive results than Mencken—I think immediately of Lewis Mumford or of Edmund Wilson. But no one in twentieth century America has done it with more verve and dash than Mencken. His energy, his humor, his irreverence, his satiric bite, and even some of his prejudices can still be refreshing and exciting. Fortunately, however, there is more to Mencken than the noise and fireworks. Beneath the flash and thunder of his satiric prose, he envinces courage, conviction, and serious commitment to ideals.

Therefore, while Mencken may be criticized or rejected, he must be taken on his own terms if he is to be understood. Establishing those terms—looking for the unity amid the diversity of his career, searching for the real man behind the public image—is the main purpose of this book. To these ends, I have tried to write an intellectual biography of Mencken. Inevitably, such an effort is, by its nature, interpretive, and my Mencken is not necessarily the same man that other commentators have seen or will see in the future. To me Mencken was a man deeply involved with his society and his times; and he was concerned with the preservation of a set of values that, no matter how heretical he sometimes tried to make them appear, were traditionally a part of American life. In presenting this positive side of Mencken, I have, nonetheless, tried to produce a critical study in the proper meaning of that word.

Although I have tried to be as inclusive as possible in my analysis of Mencken, the brevity of this study, the breadth of the subject's interests, and, in some cases, my own limitations, have prevented me from giving complete attention to certain topics. For example, I have given less emphasis than have other writers to Mencken's association with the South. I have had to deal all too briefly with his unique and important role as a magazine editor. A proper assessment of Mencken's work in the American language is a task for someone more knowledgeable in sociolinguistics than myself. And, of course, I have been concerned with Mencken's private life only in so far as it helps in the understanding of his work and its importance.

Finally, as a cultural historian, I have taken a somewhat different approach to Mencken than I might have done had my background been primarily in literary history or criticism. My aim has been to interpret Mencken through the interaction of the man and his times. I have tried to discover to what extent he perceived the cultural problems of America, how he reacted to these problems, and how relevant and perceptive his response was to them. At the same time I have tried to suggest the role or roles he played in helping to formulate that culture in the years of his greatest influence—the period from around 1908 to the late 1920s.

While the organization of this book is essentially topical, it does roughly follow the chronology of Mencken's life. The study begins with an investigation of the influences in his early life and the importance of his early career as a journalist. Chapter 2 describes the foundation of his concept of the artist-iconoclast through his readings in Shaw, Ibsen, and Nietzsche. The ideas Mencken subsequently developed are traced through his literary criticism in the next chapter. Chapter 4 deals primarily with his social criticism in the prewar years, while the two following chapters discuss his involvement in the cultural debates of the early years of this century and his eventual disillusionment with art. Mencken's social criticism during the 1920s is the subject of Chapter 7. The next chapter tries to show the connection in Mencken's criticism between democracy and character. Chapter 9 deals with his libertarianism and his reaction to the New Deal. The last chapter attempts to resolve the various paradoxes in Mencken's work by examining the relationship between his personality and his satire.

There is one particular problem that Mencken presents to anyone attempting to write about him. The way Mencken wrote is often as important as what he wrote. I have therefore succumbed to the temptation to quote extensively from this most quotable of writers. In order to prevent the footnotes from multiplying in rabbitlike fashion, I have employed the following technique. Where the work being quoted from is referred to in the text, I have simply placed the appropriate page number in parentheses after the quotation. In some chapters where I have used a series of quotations from the same periodical or newspaper, I have included the appropriate date in the parentheses as well. In such special cases I have reminded the reader of the procedure being used in a footnote at the beginning of the chapter or section.

This book is the end product of over a decade's work on Mencken, which began when I was a graduate student in the History Department of The Johns Hopkins University. My doctoral dissertation was on Mencken, and I would like to take this opportunity to thank Professor Charles A. Barker, my supervisor at Johns Hopkins, for his patience and help over the years. I would also like to thank Professor Kenneth Lynn, who was the second reader of my dissertation, and all of the members of my examination board for their suggestions.

Among my various friends who have given me help, advice, and general encouragement in this work, I would like to thank, in particular, Dr. James B. Crooks, chairman of the History Department at Florida State University at Jacksonville; Mr. Owen Dudley Edwards of the History Department of the University of Edinburgh, Scotland; Mr. Alf MacLochlainn, director of the National Library of Ireland; and Dr. S. P. Fullinwider of the History Department of Arizona State University at Tempe. I would also like to thank Mrs. Grace B. Skinaway for typing the manuscript of this book.

Unfortunately, this book appears too late for me to express my gratitude to Miss Betty Adler, the late bibliographer of Mencken and editor of *Menckeniana* from 1962 to 1973, for her friendly help and encouragement. I am also indebted to Mr. Richard Hart, former co-chairman-in-charge of the Humanities Department of the Enoch Pratt Free Library in Baltimore, and to his staff for their help and for allowing me to use the Mencken Room, a model of its kind and a haven for visiting scholars. My thanks also to the staffs of the Manuscripts and Archives Division of the New York Public Library, the Rare Book Room of the Library of the University of Pennsylvania, and the microfilm section of the Firestone Library at Princeton University.

I am indebted also to Dr. Sylvia E. Bowman, the editor of the Twayne United States Authors Series, for her advice concerning this book, and I would like to thank her staff for their cooperation.

Finally, there are certain intangible but nonetheless real contributions to every work of this type. To my parents: thank you for helping to see me through so many years of education. To my wife, Leslie: without your encouragement at some very critical moments, this book would never have been written.

I remember with great fondness, and still a certain awe, a very pleasant and enlightening evening in the spring of 1962 which I spent with the late Mr. August Mencken, the critic's brother, at the old house at 1524 Hollins Street in Baltimore. Near the end of the evening, Mr. Mencken, who had been as generous to me with his

Jack Daniels as he had been with impressions and information, began to worry about Communists and radicals. He wondered if the John Birch Society did not have, after all, some point to their campaigns. Then looking at me with that wide-eyed glance, so characteristic of his brother, he said, with the tone of one enunciating an obvious but basic truth: "But, of course, they are *all* frauds anyway." For an instant a ghost walked through the room.

W. H. A. WILLIAMS

*Larghybrack,*
*County Donegal, Ireland*

# Acknowledgements

To Mr. William G. Frederick, vice president of the Mercantile–Safe Deposit and Trust Company, Baltimore, Maryland, for permission to quote extensively from Mencken's works, letters, and memoirs.

To Alfred Knopf and Company for permission to quote from *The American Mercury* and from the following works: *A Book of Prefaces, The American Language, Prejudices: First Series, Prejudices: Second Series, Prejudices: Third Series, Prejudices: Fourth Series, Prejudices: Fifth Series, Prejudices: Sixth Series, Notes on Democracy, Happy Days, Newspaper Days, Letters of H. L. Mencken,* edited by Guy J. Forgue, *We Moderns: Enigmas and Guesses* by Edwin Muir, and *The American Democrat* by James Fenimore Cooper.

To Mrs. Wanda M. Randall, assistant to the curator of manuscripts, Princeton University Library, Princeton, New Jersey, for permission to quote from the library's Mencken correspondence.

To Faye Simkin, executive officer of The Research Libraries, for permission to quote from the H. L. Mencken Papers, Manuscripts and Archieves Division of The New York Public Library, Astor, Lenox, and Tilden Foundations.

To Mr. William S. Forshaw, Humanities Department, Enoch Pratt Free Library, Baltimore, Maryland, and to Mr. William H. Ochs of Sussman-Ochs Company, Baltimore, Maryland, for supplying me with the copy of the photograph of Mencken used in this book.

# Chronology

1880    September 12: Henry Louis Mencken born, Baltimore, Maryland.
1896    Graduates valedictorian from Baltimore Polytechnic Institute; end of formal education.
1899    Begins career in journalism as cub reporter on the Baltimore *Morning Herald*.
1903    City editor on the *Herald*.
1905    Managing editor of the *Herald;* publishes first book, *George Bernard Shaw: His Plays*.
1906    Begins association with the Baltimore *Sunpapers*.
1908    Publishes *Philosophy of Friedrich Nietzsche;* begins reviewing books for the *Smart Set;* meets Theodore Dreiser and George Jean Nathan.
1910    Publishes *Men Versus the Man*, written with R. R. La Monte.
1911    Begins the daily "Free Lance" column in the *Evening Sun*.
1912    First trip to Europe.
1913    Writes "The American" series for the *Smart Set;* with George Jean Nathan assists Willard Huntington Wright in editing the magazine.
1914    Co-editor of the *Smart Set* with Nathan.
1915    End of the "Free Lance" due to anti-German feeling.
1916    Trip to the eastern front for the *Sunpapers*.
1917    Suspends work for the *Sunpapers;* publishes first book of criticism, *A Book of Prefaces*.
1918    Publishes *In Defense of Women*.
1919    Publishes first edition of *The American Language; Prejudices: First Series*.
1920    Returns to *Sunpapers* with weekly series of articles.
1923    Leaves the *Smart Set*.

1924    With Nathan, founds *The American Mercury*.

1925    Sole editor of the *Mercury;* covers Scopes trial for *Sunpapers*.

1926    Publishes *Notes On Democracy*.

1927    Brings out sixth and last book of the *Prejudices* series.

1930    Marries Sara Haardt; publishes *Treatise on the Gods*.

1934    Resigns editorship of the *Mercury*.

1936    Brings out fourth revised edition of *The American Language*.

1938    End of the weekly articles in the *Evening Sun;* February 8 to May 7: acting editor of the *Evening Sun*.

1940    Publishes *Happy Days*, the first of three volumes of memoirs.

1941    Ceases writing for the *Sunpapers;* remains on payroll.

1945    Brings out *Supplement I* to *The American Language*.

1948    Resumes writing for *Sunpapers; Supplement II* of *The American Language;* suffers stroke; end of career.

1956    January 29: dies at Baltimore.

# CHAPTER 1

# *The Making of an Iconoclast*

## I  *Home*

A home is not a mere transient shelter: its essence lies in its permanence, in its capacity for accretion and solidification, in its quality of representing, in all its details, the personalities of the people who live in it. . . . I have lived in the one house in Baltimore for nearly forty-five years. . . . If I had to leave it I'd be as certainly crippled as if I lost a leg."[1] Written during the 1920s, when H. L. Mencken's reputation as a satirist, a skeptic, and, indeed, a cynic was at its height, his apotheosis of so traditional an institution as the home must have struck some of his readers as quite out of character. Yet no rebel was ever more conventionally and securely rooted. Three years after his birth on September 12, 1880, Mencken's family moved into the red brick house at 1524 Hollins Street, Baltimore, Maryland; and, with the exception of the five years of his marriage, Mencken lived there until his death in 1956.

From this comfortable, middle class home, Mencken's roots extended into the city of Baltimore, which even twenty years of editing work in New York could never tempt him to leave. Writing in 1913 about the Baltimorean, Mencken summarized his own need to belong to one place. "There is a simplicity about him . . . which speaks of long habituation to his own opinions, his own dignities, his own class. In a country so largely dynamic and so little static that few of its people ever seem (or are) quite at home in their own homes, [the Baltimorean] represents a more settled and a more stately order."[2]

Mencken professed to see some of the virtues of the old Colonial planter in the Baltimore character, and some of the city's Southern qualities appealed to him. Yet, even in Mencken's day, Southern charm and pace were inexorably mixed with the industrialism and ethnically variegated population typical of Northern cities. The citizen of a border city in a border state, Mencken was no more a Southerner than he was a Yankee. Although he later had a special interest in the culture of the South, Mencken had little actual experience with the real South. In fact, except for occasional excursions into the Maryland countryside, Mencken's youth was bounded by the city limits of Baltimore.[3]

Essentially, Mencken was an urbanite. He was one of the first American critics to champion the values of the city over those of rural America. If some of his supposedly urban values have a slightly bucolic ring about them today, this appeal is not due to any real "Southernness" in Mencken's makeup. Rather, it can be traced to the fact that Baltimore in the 1880s was still in the process of industrializing and retained, therefore, something of the atmosphere of its earlier preindustrial days.

Mencken's heritage was primarily ethnic, not regional. Both of his grandfathers came to America from Germany in 1848, not as fleeing revolutionaries, but simply as men in search of economic opportunity. Grandfather Burkhardt Ludwig Mencken, a certified tobacconist, founded the family cigar business in Baltimore; and Henry remembered him as a bearded patriarch who ruled the Mencken family with the firm hand typical of the German *Bürger*. Neither Henry's grandfather nor father, however, took an active interest in the German-American community in the city. Although Henry received some instruction in the German language, it was not spoken in the home. In fact, the influence of his ethnic background on his early life does not seem to have been especially dominant. During his youth, it seems to have manifested itself more in terms of a strong home life and in family pride rather than in ethnic separateness. Mencken's German-Americanism was more important as a factor that shaped his cultural rebellion than as a source for that rebellion.[4]

Henry's father August, devoted to his family, his firm, and his baseball team, appears to have been a typical American businessman of the late nineteenth century. A high-tariff Democrat, August held no-nonsense views on free silver radicalism and passed on to this eldest son the economic and social conservatism of the petit bourgeois entrepreneur. Despite the father's influence, the dominant personality in the household was Mencken's mother, Anna Abhau Mencken, who lived at Hollins Street until her death in

1925. The adult H. L. Mencken may have shaken the world of literary criticism and hurled his satirical dead cats at presidents, but at home his mother ruled with unquestioned authority. Mencken was very close to her, and she was the center of that domestic life that was so important to him. It is significant that he remained a bachelor until he was fifty, five years after her death.

In the 1940s, when Mencken wrote his charming memoirs, he entitled the volume dealing with his boyhood, *Happy Days*. Certainly, no biographer has yet uncovered any evidence that suggests that Mencken's early years were anything but what he himself called "placid, secure, uneventful and happy." The Mencken children were "encapsulated in affection" and kept "fat, saucy and contented" (vii). In only one respect does the Mencken family seem to have deviated slightly from the American middle class norm of the period. As Mencken put it in 1939, "Religion was simply not a living subject in the house. It was discussed now and then but only as astro-physics might have been discussed. I grew up believing that it was unimportant and I am still of that opinion."[5] Although a basic element in Mencken's philosophy, agnosticism was not the product of a rebellion against home and church. Rather, it was a part of that complex bundle of attitudes and prejudices that Mencken fashioned from out of his family background.

As a boy, Mencken seems to have differed from the majority of his contemporaries of his class only in his prodigious reading. During his teens, he read William Makepeace Thackery, Joseph Addison, Sir Richard Steele, Alexander Pope, Samuel Johnson, Thomas Babington Macaulay, Lord Byron, Rudyard Kipling, William Dean Howells, Henry James, and Stephen Crane. "Altogether, I doubt that any human being in this world has ever read more than I did between my twelfth and eighteenth years."[6] In the process he made his first literary "discovery"; for Mark Twain's *The Adventures of Huckleberry Finn* made such an impression on him as a boy that he reread it annually until he was forty. Appropriately, Mencken was one of the first critics to hail Twain as a great artist.[7]

In spite of young Mencken's literary interests, he was also fascinated by science. He attended the Baltimore Polytechnic Institute, a high school emphasizing science and mechanics, from which he was graduated as valedictorian in 1896. By this time, however, letters had won the tug of war with science for Mencken's mind; and he announced to his startled family that he wanted a career in journalism. The result was a sharp conflict with his father, for August Mencken had his own plans for his son. Henry could study law at the University of Maryland, enroll in The Johns Hopkins University, or, and here parental pressure was strongest, enter the family tobacco business. Since Polytechnic's valedictorian had had enough of pedagogues and classrooms, and since he was barred from journalism, he unenthusiastically began to learn the dreary rudiments of the cigar trade.

The next months were unhappy ones for young Mencken. "The very idea of selling revolted me," he later recalled. "I never got over my loathing."[8] Secretly he took a correspondence course in writing and dreamed of the exciting career of a newspaperman. Although his mother was sympathetic, August Mencken remained adamant against journalism, and Henry could not bring himself to rebel against his father. Then, suddenly, the crisis was resolved with awful finality. "My father died on Friday, January 13, 1899," he noted in *Newspaper Days*. "On the Monday evening immediately following [the funeral], . . . I presented myself in the city-room of the old Baltimore *Morning Herald* and applied to Max Ways, the city editor, for a job on his staff" (3).

Mencken's persistent pursuit of a career in journalism was an act of rebellion directed not so much against his father, but rather against certain aspects of the bourgeois world that had nurtured him so well. Few careers deviated more from the respectable norm of that of a middle class businessman than what Mencken himself dubbed in *Newspaper Days* as the "maddest, gladdest, damndest existence ever enjoyed by mortal youth"—the world of the turn of the century reporter (ix). At its gaudiest pinnacle, this career promised the romantic adventures of a Richard Harding Davis or a George Stevens. On its everyday level, journalism offered the colorful earthiness and excitement of night courts, waterfront brawls, and political rallies. As Mencken wrote in *Newspaper Days*, "at a time when the respectable bourgeois youngsters of my generation were college freshmen, . . . affronted      with      balderdash . . . by      chalky pedagogues, I was at large in a wicked seaport of half a million people, . . . getting earfuls and eyefuls of instruction in a hundred giddy arcana, none of them taught in schools" (ix).

Mencken's venture into journalism, then, was a rebellion against the middle class insistence on gentility in culture and on respectability in professions. The door to Max Way's office was an entrance into a new world and an escape from an old one. Yet the door was never fully closed behind Mencken. His was a half way rebellion. If he rejected the surface of middle class life, he was to cling tenaciously to its essentials. Although he would satirize bourgeois mores, Mencken took with him into journalism the discipline, the ambition, and the basic values of his class.

The influence of Mencken's background upon his later iconoclasm is paradoxical. Apart from the single, although important, incident of the clash with his father over his career, the ransacking of Mencken's youth in search for trauma, maladjustment, nonconformity—the tell-tale signs of the rebel in the making—is an unrewarding and probably misleading task. The stable, prosperous, confident bourgeois atmosphere in which he grew up was *itself* the dominating influence upon his development as an iconoclast. The strength of Mencken's roots in his home and his environment gave him the overwhelming self-confidence necessary for his later onslaughts against his society. In a period when so many American writers were to pursue the theme of "you can't go home again," Mencken used the psychological security of "home" as a basis from which to launch the barbs of his satire.

## II  *Journalism*

Mencken's early experience as a journalist influenced him in several important ways, not the least of which was the reinforcement it gave to his already strong sense of self-assurance. Six years after he began working on the *Morning Herald* as a cub reporter, he had risen at the age of twenty-five to become the paper's managing editor. By then he had experienced practically every type of work the paper had to offer, from reporting, reviewing, and feature writing to editing. Mencken thus enjoyed the kind of rapid success that according to the myth of American individualism, was the just reward for hard work and talent. It is little wonder that he never really questioned the basic tenets of this myth and was to dedicate so much of his later writing to its defense.

Certainly, if Mencken's own statements are to be believed, no one was more self-consciously individualistic than the old-time journalist. In *Newspaper Days*, he claimed that the journalist saw himself as "a free spirit and darling of the gods, licensed by his high merits to ride and deride the visible universe . . ."(xi). Very often the visible universe under the newspaperman's nose was the rather sordid one of poverty, crime, prostitution, and political corruption. It was a rough training ground for a youthful mind, and to some extent Mencken's philosophical Naturalism, like that of Theodore Dreiser and Stephen Crane, can be traced to the very unidealistic view of life seen on and from the reporter's beat.

There were other aspects of turn of the century journalism that played a more creative role in Mencken's development. "The daily newspaper," said novelist David Graham Phillips, "sustains the same relation to the young writer as the hospital to the medical student."[9] The challenge of grasping and holding the attention of readers as they bolted their morning coffee often forced journalists to develop a colorful, racy style and an abrasive sense of humor. Unlike the middle class magazines, with their genteel, largely feminine audience, the daily urban paper had a predominantly male readership that delighted in the dramatic, the satirical and the vituperative.

The newspaperman was so freed from some of the taboos and restraints of genteel journalism that even the language he employed often reflected the tart slang of the streets where he found his material. At a time when the universities and the "respectable" press were trying to maintain the English standard in American speech, writers like Finley Peter Dunne, George Ade, and Ring Lardner employed the urban patois of immigrants, Negroes, and sports figures. Creating a new brand of satire, these writers sought to unmask the foibles of their times through the use of dialect and slang.

Mencken was particularly impressed by George Ade and for a time tried to write his own imitations of Ade's "Fables in Slang."[10] Although the results were unimpressive, Mencken, like Ade, Dunne, and also Ambrose Bierce, learned to exploit the gap between "cultured" speech and the vernacular of the people. Much of the success of Mencken's satire depended upon dropping a pompous academic phrase into an ordinary sentence or exploding a slang term amid a line of ponderous latinate words. The humor sprang from the contrast between respectable and so-called unrespectable colloquial forms of speech. As one commentator has observed, such writing was a playing in the linguistic waters "where two strong currents, Standard and American English, met. . . ."[11] Mencken's allegiance lay with the American vernacular. The origins of his pioneeering work, *The American Language*, are to be found in some of his early columns for the Baltimore *Sun* in which he delighted in publishing examples of pungent Baltimorese, which he had begun collecting while still a reporter.

Another journalistic influence that Mencken absorbed contributed directly to his development as a literary critic. During the 1890s there emerged from the ranks of the journalists a small group of critics, who rejected the predominating genteel opinion that insisted that literature and art had to reflect American moralism and idealism. At war with the Genteel Tradition, these journalist-critics turned their backs on the universities and the conservative publishing houses and looked to the avant garde, particularly in Europe, to satisfy their yearnings for new departures in art. Prophets of Naturalism and apostles of Estheticism (although seldom Decadence), men like Percival Pollard, Vance Thompson, William Marion Reedy, James Gibbons Huneker, and Ambrose Bierce played an important role in helping to introduce Americans to the latest developments in art. Mencken, who personally knew Pollard, Huneker, and Bierce, was in this tradition. Indeed, "An unbroken line of newspaper iconoclasts stretches all the way from the pale aesthetes of the nineties to a surprising, improbable conclusion in H. L. Mencken."[12]

From the journalist-critics Mencken picked up the style of Impressionism. Enamored with neither objectivity nor academic formalism, the critic was completely subjective; he recorded his own personal reaction—his impressions—of the work of art; and his purpose was to make art come alive for the viewer or reader. As Mencken himself once explained, the critic was the "catalyst" between art and the public. If the critic managed to entertain in the process, so much the better; for style was as important as ideas. Moreover, Mencken also followed his mentors in their assumption that the artist of genius was usually in a state of war with conventional society. Although Mencken did not accept the "art for art's sake" doctrine held by some of the critics of the 1890s, he did posit a connection between art and iconoclasm, a point discussed in the next chapter.

Essentially, journalism provided Mencken with a training and a tradition quite at variance with what he would have received had he taken his father's offer of a university education. In 1900, the universities were custodians of a nineteenth century Victorian culture that was becoming increasingly irrelevant to an urbanizing, industrial America that had a vast immigrant population. In the face of this raw, dynamic, but also troubled America, the universities along with other bastions of the Genteel Tradition preached a concept of art that either looked back to a simpler rural past or celebrated a noble idealism that was often sadly out of touch with reality. Genteel critics often tended to condemn or ignore contemporary art which called into question this idealism.

All of the influences that journalism brought to bear on Mencken were antagonistic toward this Genteel Tradition and its culture of idealism. If the first stage of Mencken's rebellion was the choice of a career in journalism, then the second, his development as an iconoclast, was a consequence of that choice.

CHAPTER 2

# The Artist-Iconoclast: 1905–1909

WHILE journalism had an important influence on Mencken's development as a cultural rebel, his rejection of a university education probably deprived his mind of the formal, rigorous training that would have added depth to his thinking. Although he was extremely well read in several fields and pursued wide-ranging interests, Mencken never acquired the ability (or, perhaps, the desire) to penetrate far below the surface of ideas. Although he liked to call himself a "critic of ideas," he was really more of a collector than an analyst of ideas. His mind always reflected the traits of the self-made intellectual: oversimplification, overconfidence, and rigidity. Throughout his life, he considered it a sign of strength that he seldom changed his ideas and opinions.

Nevertheless, Mencken was a pioneer. He helped to introduce and popularize writers, native and foreign, who were either unknown or deserved a wider hearing. Moreover, the man's energy and enthusiasm were astounding. Between 1905 and 1908, he published the *first* book about George Bernard Shaw, the *first* popular work about Friedrich Nietzsche, and several interesting essays on Henrik Ibsen; he established a reputation as a promising critic; and he all the while continued his work as a newspaperman. Although the very spread and variety of his work warns against expecting very much depth, his writings on Shaw, Ibsen, and Nietzsche are important. Because these books helped to break new ground, they are documents in American cultural history. At the same time, they help us trace in Mencken's criticism the evolution of the concept of the artist-iconoclast.

## I  Theater and Iconoclasm

As a critic, Mencken is best remembered for his astringent comments on the American novel. Nevertheless, he first entered the

25

arena of criticism through the stage door when he became drama editor for the *Herald* in 1901. After moving to the Baltimore *Sun-papers* in 1906, he continued reviewing plays for the next three years. He stopped reviewing, according to his own testimony, as an act of mercy toward the local theater managers, who complained of his scathing notices.[1]

In spite of Baltimore's provinciality (or, perhaps, because of it), the city in those days was a favorite place for pre-Broadway trial runs. Mencken, therefore, had an opportunity to sample a wide selection of American dramatic fare, but most of what he saw earned his contempt because few native playwrights in the early years of this century rose above the level of conventional competence. Dramatists like Bronson Howard, Augustus Thomas, Clyde Fitch, and William Vaughn Moody made some notable efforts to draw the American theater away from its endless diet of stereotyped historical plays, sentimental melodramas, and superficial comedies. Their attempts to come to grips with the reality of American life were, unfortunately, all too modest. As Alan S. Downer has asserted, "even the best of serious plays written by Americans before the first World War are not more than superficially true to life. . . ."[2] It is little wonder that Mencken found more vitality in the irreverent burlesque sketches of Joe Weber and Lew Fields, a source for his own style of humor.[3]

Even in his early reviews, Mencken demanded Realism from both the playwrights and the actors. He wanted the theater to be "a field of action for personages resembling, in thought and act, the men and women we see about us every day."[4] Bored with Romantic fantasy and the Victorian conventions of the well-made play, Mencken sought inspiration from the theater of ideas that had emerged in Europe during the late nineteenth century. In his own words he wanted to see "human beings at their tricks; to witness combats between will and will, idea and idea, faith and faith, ideal and ideal; to attend a psychological peep show."[5] Nonetheless, Mencken's hopes for the modern theater went beyond the techniques of Realism and Naturalism. As he read writers like Ibsen and Shaw, he noted that in their dramatic presentations of the relationship between man and his society, they brought into question many traditional middle class beliefs, conventions, and values. He began to conceive the theater as a medium for iconoclasm. On stage, the veil of sanctity and sentimentality would be stripped away from human institutions and customs, exposing them to the cold light of inquiry and doubt.

This conception of the artist as an iconoclast is the essential idea behind Mencken's presentation of both Shaw and Ibsen. Mencken's *George Bernard Shaw: His Plays,* which was published in 1905, was essentially a guide book to Shaw's works; but Mencken also sought to provide an interpretation of the playwright's position as both an artist and a thinker. He placed Shaw within the context of what he took to be the most important development of the nineteenth century: the gradual triumph of intellectual freedom over religious and secular orthodoxies. In a very simplistic reading of intellectual history, Mencken presented Charles Darwin as the key figure in this process of liberation. He began his book, then, not with the dramatist but with the evolutionist.

Before Darwin, Mencken claimed in *Shaw,* "One had to believe or be damned. There was no compromise and no middle ground" (x). With the publication of *The Origin of Species,* however, "Ramparts of authority that had resisted doubts fell like hedge-rows before the facts. . . . For six thousand years it had been necessary, in defending a doctrine, to show only that it was respectable or sacred. Since 1859, it has been needful to prove its truth" (xi). Although Darwin was dead, the spirit of the Darwinian liberation continued. "Thomas Huxley and Herbert Spencer, like a new Ham and a new Shem, spend their lives seeing to that. From [Darwin] through Huxley, we have . . . our affable indifference to hell. Through Spencer . . . we have Nietzsche, Sudermann, Hauptmann, Ibsen . . . and the aforesaid George Bernard Shaw" (ix–x). For Mencken, Shaw's importance lay in his satirical challenge to conventional thought. Mencken divided the characters in Shaw's plays into two categories: "the ordinary folks who represent the great majority, and the iconoclasts . . ." (xvi). Shaw himself was the perfect iconoclast: "Either he is exhibiting a virtue as a vice in disguise, or exhibiting a vice as a virtue in vice's clothing. In this fact lies the excuse for considering him a world-figure" (xii).

Prior to writing about Shaw, Mencken had become interested in the plays of Henrik Ibsen. During this period, Mencken collaborated with a friend, the Danish consul in Baltimore, to produce a new translation of some of Ibsen's plays into the American idiom. Two, *A Doll's House* and *Little Eyolf,* were published in 1909 with Mencken's introductions. Although Darwin does not appear in

Mencken's introduction to *A Doll's House*, he still viewed modern theater in terms of the liberation of society from the chains of orthodoxy; and he viewed this play as one of those works that helped men throw off the "crushing heritage of formalism and tradition, in art as well as in living . . ." (vi). Ibsen's play was important in its day because, by criticizing so sacrosanct an institution as marriage, it "served to prepare the way for an advance in human thought" (xii).

From Mencken's writings on Shaw, Ibsen, and, later, Nietzsche emerge the features of his ideal cultural hero: the artist-iconoclast. This concept, which coupled art and iconoclasm, dominated much of Mencken's early criticism, but it was not the result of an esthetic theory. Rather, it stemmed from a conviction on Mencken's part that art had a vital role to play in society. In 1909 he explained that, "As a matter of fact, the world gets ahead by losing its illusions, and not by fostering them. Nothing, perhaps, is more painful than disillusion, but all the same, nothing is more necessary. . . . Because a horde of impious critics hang upon the flanks of our dearest beliefs today, our children, five hundred years hence, will be free from our present firm faith in political panaceas, unlucky days, dreams, hunches and the influence of mind over matter. Disillusion is like quinine. Its taste is abominable—but it cures."[6] The artist functioned iconoclastically by bringing into damning juxtaposition faith and reason, convention and reality. By causing people to question their beliefs, the artist cleared the way for a more rational society. For this reason, Mencken, in holding up Shaw as a model iconoclast, could state, "Such a man, I believe, does a lot of good in the world." He was an enemy to all "vile impediments to human progress."[7]

Mencken conceived his artist-iconoclast in the most romantic and idealistic terms. He was to be a sort of intellectual pioneer by blazing trails into the future, by felling the shibboleths of outworn creeds and ideas, and by clearing away the obstacles to the development of a rational, enlightened society. Because of Mencken's youthful enthusiasm, however, he unwittingly involved himself in a serious contradiction. He gave his iconoclast the negative power to attack error but witheld from him the positive function of building on the ruins of error. "A preacher necessarily endeavors to make all his hearers think exactly as he does," Mencken insisted in *Shaw*. "A dramatist merely tries to make them think. The nature of their conclusions is of minor consequence" (xxiv). The business of the artist was simply to "record the facts of life as he sees them" so that the public would "deduce therefrom new rules of human conduct. . ." (xiv).

In suggesting that the artist was to force society to rethink its values and institutions but not to help it shape new ones, Mencken was trying to avoid what he considered to be the established pitfalls of American criticism. He clearly rejected the "art for art's sake" doctrine of the esthetes of the 1890s. At the same time, he wanted desperately to liberate American art from the Genteel Tradition's dictum that didacticism, not criticism, was the essential function of good art. Mencken knew that, when the artist turned propagandist or tractarian, his art often suffered. Therefore, he wanted his artist-iconoclast to have a social function *and* at the same time to remain true to his art. Mencken's artist, therefore, had both a creative and a social role. The causual connection between the two, however, rested on Mencken's uncritical faith that art and intellect, creativity and truth-seeking, iconoclasm and progress were invariably bound together as natural allies in the long struggle of the human mind against obscurantism. When this faith began to crumble, so did Mencken's confidence in the union of art and iconoclasm.

## II  *Darwinizing Nietzsche*

Mencken's writings on Shaw and Ibsen developed naturally from his own interests and experiences. His work on the German philosopher, Friedrich Nietzsche, began, on the other hand, as a simple business proposition. In 1906, when the publishers of *Shaw* asked Mencken to try his hand at a volume about Nietzsche, Mencken agreed: and the result, *The Philosophy of Friedrich Nietzsche*, was published in 1908. The book was a moderate success, and Mencken brought out a new, revised edition in 1913.[8] For the next decade this book remained such an important source for the young intellectuals that, during the early 1920s, *Vanity Fair* twice cited Mencken in its "Hall of Fame" for having "contributed more to the popular understanding of Nietzsche than any other American."[9]

"Understanding" is not, perhaps, the most apt word. The Nietzsche that Mencken gave to American readers was often nothing more than Mencken himself, in the disguise of the German philosopher. This factor in itself is not too damning, for Nietzsche's writings are still considered difficult and controversial. Moreover, most of those few Americans who turned to Nietzsche in the prewar

years treated his works like a philosophical ragbag from which they
carefully selected the appropriate aphorisms to support their own
presuppositions. As a result, Nietzsche appeared in such unlikely
guises as a liberal Christian or even a Marxist. At least Mencken's
insistence on presenting Nietzsche as an enemy of Christianity,
democracy, and middle class idealism conveyed something of the
authentic voice of the German.[10]

Because Nietzsche's philosophy denied so many basic American
values, Mencken faced a formidable task in trying to make him
palatable to an American audience. At the time of Nietzsche's death
in 1900, the *New York Times* had dismissed the idea that he was a
serious philosopher as "preposterous" and had compared him to the
"devil-worshippers" of Paris. Mencken's task as a popularizer was to
find, both for his audience and for himself, some familiar frame of
reference within which Nietzsche might be fitted. Mencken did so
by forcing the German into the one mode of American popular
thought that Mencken himself enthusiastically accepted: Social
Darwinism. By Darwinizing Nietzsche, Mencken also Americanized him.[11]

As a teenager, Mencken had absorbed many of the Social Darwinian attitudes of the late nineteenth century. He had cut his intellectual eyeteeth on such Darwinian apostles as Thomas Huxley and
Herbert Spencer, but he had been especially impressed by William
Graham Sumner and had retained a lifelong admiration for his
works.[12] As a result, Mencken accepted unconditionally the concept
of progress through competition. He firmly believed that "we are
still being driven forward and upward, unceasingly and willy-nilly,
by the irresistible operation of the law of natural selection."[13] The
idea of the struggle for existence so captured Mencken's imagination
that he proclaimed in his book on Nietzsche: "If victory comes not,
let it be defeat, death and annihilation—but, in any event, let there
be a fair fight. Without this constant strife—this constant testing—
this constant elimination of the unfit—there can be no progress"
(105).

Mencken romanticized the Darwinian struggle for existence because he conceived it in intellectual, and not just social and
economic, terms. The joy of the "highest caste man," he wrote, was
to be found "in effort, in work, in progress. A difficulty overcome, a
riddle solved, . . . a fact proved, an error destroyed. . . ."
Mencken's Social Darwinism was, therefore, something more than

an apologia for capitalism. "My own private view . . . is that the idea of truth-seeking will one day take the place of the idea of money-making."[14] In this way Mencken managed to turn the Darwinian concept of the struggle for existence into the iconoclast's attack on orthodoxy. He viewed Nietzsche, therefore, through the twin lenses of Darwinism and iconoclasm.

The best illustration of this approach is Mencken's interpretation of Nietzsche's famous cultural dualism: the apposition of the mythical figures of Apollo and Dionysus. Nietzsche felt there were two forces in life: the Apollonian, which was philosophical and contemplative, and the Dionysian or the dynamic element. Mencken blurred the many subtle distinctions between the two. The Apollonian spirit appeared to him to be nothing more than the timid conservative's defense of the intellectual status quo, while he conceived of the Dionysian spirit in terms of iconoclastic rebellion. Or, as he stated in *Nietzsche,* "the apollonians . . . stood for permanence and the dionysians . . . stood for change." The former insisted on a "strict obedience to certain invariable rules, which found expression as religion, law, and morality." The aim of the latter was to "adapt themselves to changing circumstances, and to avoid the snares of artificial, permanent rules" (72).

Nietzsche, of course, had not given unqualified assent to either Apollo or Dionysus. His great purpose, which he achieved in his later works, was to develop a synthesis of the two forces. Mencken may have been vaguely aware that the philosopher had sought such a balance, but he clearly admired what he took to be the superior and more vital virtues of Dionysus. In *Nietzsche* he claimed, "Dionysus may fall short of triumph to the end of the chapter, but so long as he wages his war upon Apollo fiercely and intelligently there need be no fear of the perils of sloth, of vegetation, of bigotry, of authority, of standing still. . . . Today, the preacher who thunders from the pulpit and the statesman who howls from the rostrum must take thought of and give heed to the doubter who arises in his place and demands to know wherefore and why" (293–94, 1908).

Mencken was less interested in understanding the essence of Nietzsche's philosophy than he was in extolling the ruggedly individualistic gospel of Rooseveltian strenuosity. Indeed, he even insisted that Nietzsche's philosophy was identical to that expressed by Theodore Roosevelt in *The Strenuous Life.* Commenting in *Nietzsche* on Roosevelt's philosophy, Mencken wrote, "There is no denial of the law of natural selection in this thunderous sermon of the American dionysian . . ." (271, 1908). Summarizing the philosophy of his Darwinized (and thus Americanized) Nietzsche, Mencken called it the "gospel of prudent and intelligent selfishness, of absolute and utter individualism" (102).

This extreme individualism colors Mencken's attempt to explain Nietzsche's concept of the *Übermensch*. Mencken totally missed the poetic ecstasy of the philosopher's vision—what Nietzsche called the "urge toward unity, a reaching out beyond person . . . reality, beyond the abyss of perishing."[15] Anxious to present the German as a practical philosopher with both feet planted firmly in reality, Mencken played down his Zarathustrian prophesies about the *Übermensch*. As far as Mencken was concerned, Nietzsche's superman was "merely man raised to perfect efficiency . . . man absolutely healthy, absolutely unfettered, absolutely undeluded, absolutely immoral."[16]

Mencken was convinced that Nietzsche's concepts could lead toward the establishment of a "new aristocracy of efficiency" that would function in a state of "ideal anarchy." As he explained in *Nietzsche*, under such conditions the world would witness the ascendancy of powerful figures, such as Abraham Lincoln, Otto von Bismark, Darwin, and Huxley, who were the "Sham-smashers and truth-tellers and mob-fighters" (198). Such men would "re-establish the law of natural selection firmly upon its disputed throne, and so the strong would grow ever stronger and more efficient, and the weak would grow ever more obedient and tractile" (197).

The emotional and psychological storm center flashing behind Nietzsche's work was totally lost upon Mencken. He was poorly equipped, both philosophically and temperamentally, to understand the Existentialist side of the German's thought. Comfortably and uncritically immersed in Social Darwinism and a firm believer in progress, Mencken was completely insensitive to the spiritual crisis of the nineteenth century intellectuals who had agonized over the challenge that science and materialism had presented to the metaphysical and spiritual side of their culture. Missing the sense of crisis, Mencken missed the heart of Nietzschhhe's work and found it relatively easy to gloss over the fact that the philosopher had once condemned Darwin as a "nihilist."

Mencken *used* Nietzsche, as he used Shaw and Ibsen and almost every writer he ever championed; for the philosopher became another model of the perfect iconoclast whose mission, as Mencken explained in *Nietzsche*, was "to attack error wherever he saw it and to proclaim truth wherever he found it. It is only by such iconoclasm and proselyting that humanity can be helped" (201). Nietzsche, Mencken insisted, had been a fighter against the "only real crime in the world . . . unreasoning belief" (4). Instinctively, Mencken also sought to use Nietzsche to shore up Social Darwinism against the stresses of its own inner contradictions. No philosophy, not even the loose and informal doctrines of American Social Darwinism, could long maintain in combination such contradictory elements as naturalistic determinism, laissez-faire economics, Protestant idealism, and native individualism. By the turn of the century, Social Darwinism was beginning to break apart as an intellectual force. The harsh competiveness and extreme individualism of Sumner and the benign determinism of Spencer were being replaced by a more liberal emphasis on cooperation and intervention—what Richard Hofstadter called the "transition towards solidarism" and Eric Goldman denoted as "Reform Darwinism."[17]

Mencken believed, however, as he wrote in *Nietzsche*, that progress could result only from the triumph of "those strong, free, self-reliant, resourceful men whose capacities are so much greater than the mob's that they are often able to force their ideas upon it . . ." (197). He wanted to turn Social Darwinism into an apologia for pure elitism. His purpose in trying to graft what he took from Nietzsche onto the Darwinian branch was to use the former to purify the latter by reestablishing individualism at the center of social philosophy. Nietzsche helped Mencken rid Social Darwinism of the "corrupting" influences of Christian altruism and Progressive idealism. At the same time, Mecken sought to arm Nietzscheanism with the Darwinian weapons of the struggle for existence and the law of natural selection, which he hoped would provide the liberating force for his aristocracy of iconoclasts.

On the surface, Nietzsche served Mencken well. Having convinced himself that the iconoclast was the harbinger of progress, Mencken obviously sought to fit himself into this mold. To do so successfully, he needed to feel himself and present himself as a member of the intellectual vanguard. His work on Shaw, Ibsen, and especially Nietzsche helped him to force his way into the forefront of the cultural debates in America.

Mencken's encounter with Nietzsche also helped him to put his ideas into a roughly consistent, if limited and highly simplistic, framework. It is true, as D. C. Stenerson has shown, that most of Mencken's "prejudices" had already been formed by the time he had completed his apprenticeship as a journalist and well before he started work on the philosopher.[18] Without Nietzsche, however, Mencken might have never risen above the level of a local newspaper sage to have gained a national reputation. Nietzsche, a catalyst for Mencken, helped him to order and solidify his own ideas.

In the end, the quality of those ideas disturbs the reader more than the distortions of Nietzsche's thought; but Mencken's Darwinized Nietzsche gave him the nearest thing he would ever have to an ideology. Mencken viewed society in terms of the eternal struggle between the talented individual and the ignorant, venal mob. This conflict contained certain dramatic possibilities that Mencken certainly exploited in his satire. As to whether or not this stark and crudely simple approach would be enough to enable Mencken to understand the complex and rapidly changing American society that would occupy so much of his attention—this question was not yet a crucial one for him in 1908. The initial importance of his book on Nietzsche was that it clearly stamped Mencken as a cultural rebel. Nietzsche, no matter how garbled, was a challenge to American thought, especially to Genteel idealism. The final rebellion that was to overthrow the Genteel Tradition was only beginning in 1908. As Henry F. May has noted, with Mencken's book "a lonely glove was thrown down and a whole period of revolution foreshadowed."[19]

CHAPTER 3

# The Literary Critic

The period between 1908 and the outbreak of World War I was one of the most decisive in Mencken's career. In those half dozen years he solidified his satirical style, laid the basis for a national reputation as a literary critic, and, through his constant journalistic commentary on his society, arrived at a thoroughly dissenting view of America. The two key developments in this period were his association with the *Smart Set* magazine, beginning in 1908, and the establishment of his signed daily column, "The Free Lance," in the Baltimore *Evening Sun* in 1911. In this chapter, which concerns Mencken the literary critic, the focus is primarily on his prewar essays. In order to avoid repetition later on, however, his comments on the novel and on criticism are traced into the 1920s. The following chapter deals with his social and cultural criticism of America prior to World War I. One should bear in mind, however, that any rigid compartmentalization of Mencken's work can be misleading. The same concern for the development of American culture and the quality of life in America informs everything he wrote.

In the spring of 1908 Mencken was invited to write the book review section for the *Smart Set*, a monthly magazine with a dubious reputation. A somewhat tarnished remnant of New York's *fin de siècle* days, the *Smart Set* was founded in 1900 by the self-styled Colonel William D'Alton Mann, an ambitious publishing buccaneer and scandlemonger. The magazine was the outgrowth of an earlier periodical, *Town Topics*, which successfully combined literary Bohemianism and international *bon vivant* criticism with spicy gossip concerning New York's "four hundred." Eventually freed from the colonel's activities, if not from the taint of his reputation, the *Smart Set* published such authors as O. Henry, Clyde Fitch, David Belasco, James Branch Cabell, Frank Norris, Jack London, Edgar Saltus, and Continental writers such as Anatole France.[1]

With its tradition of combining works of solid literary merit with a light sophisticated touch, the *Smart Set* was ideally suited to Mencken's uninhibited satirical style and unacademic approach to literature. Moreover, his work on the magazine brought him into contact with George Jean Nathan, a young drama critic who shared many of Mencken's tastes and who was to become his alter ego in one of the most famous editorial partnerships in American magazine history.

In retrospect, the year 1908 can be seen as the beginning of a new departure from the dominance of the Genteel Tradition in American criticism. In addition to Mencken's and Nathan's debuts in the *Smart Set* (and Mencken's book on Nietzsche), the year also saw the publication of Van Wyck Brooks' first book, *The Wine of the Puritans*. Dissent also came from more conservative quarters with the appearance of Irving Babbitt's *Literature and the American College*. Also in 1908, Babbitt's fellow Humanist, Paul Elmer More, was preparing to exchange his position as literary editor of the New York *Evening Post* for the editorship of the more influential magazine, the *Nation*.

That the first decade of the new century should have ended with the emergence of so many new and divergent voices in criticism can be explained, in part, by the comparative paucity of good writing in America. Unlike the decades that bracket it, the period from 1900 to 1910 was neither exciting nor momentous for the American novel. True, the style of Realism continued to gain acceptance. Moreover, some writers made genuine attempts to come to grips with the economic and social realities of life in the early years of the Progressive era. Nonetheless, the artistic results were seldom impressive. Except for the work of Henry James, who was living in England and who was not highly regarded at home, the Strenuous Age produced few books of permanent importance. Theodore Dreiser's magnificent *Sister Carrie* (1900), although not actually suppressed as legend has had it, did not make a great impact at the time. Apart from a few other notable exceptions such as Frank Norris's *The Octopus* (1901), Jack London's *The Call of the Wild* (1903), Edith Wharton's *The House of Mirth* (1905), Upton Sinclair's *The Jungle* (1906), and Gertrude Stein's *Three Women* (1909), little of permanent value was published during the decade.

Indeed, many critics of the period felt that the American novel was facing a crisis. James E. Collins, commenting in the *Bookman* in

1906, saw American writing falling into four basic categories: the "fashion plate," the "cosmic monotone," the "strenuous," and the "optimo-platitudinous." "Poverty" and "dullness" were the judgments handed down by Charles Moore in the *Dial* in 1910.[2] Contemplating the state of the American novel in 1905, a critic in the *Forum* insisted that "There is no other kind of literary work . . . in which the level of performance is so low."[3] Van Wyck Brooks mulled over the tasteless wine of the Puritans and the lack of a "constructive force" in American culture. Mencken himself characterized the situation in his own inimitable fashion in the *Smart Set* when he declared in August 1910, that "[O]ur American manufacturers of best sellers, having the souls of fudge-besotted high-school girls, behold the human comedy as a mixture of fashionable wedding and three-alarm fire, with music by Francois Frédéric Chopin . . ." (153).[4]

The defenders of the Genteel Tradition did not, of course, desire to espouse the cause of mediocrity. Some of them were painfully aware that something was wrong with the American novel, but they were trapped by their assumptions that art had to reflect not reality but the ideal, not doubt and questioning but moral and civic affirmation. They were ill-equipped to search for newer kinds of writing that would eventually revitalize American literature. As for the dissenting critics, they worked in a sort of void. There were few contemporary American writers whom they could hold up as models, and there was only a vague sense of where each critic stood in relation to his fellow rebels. Mencken, looking back on those years from the distance of 1923, recalled that there had been no concerted effort among writers and critics who were seeking to overthrow the old literary order. Each critic had to work out, more or less for himself, what was wrong with American literature and what kind of writing and imaginative insight was needed to bring in a new era.

This critical search was not, as Percy Boynton pointed out later in 1927, a purely esthetic one. "Criticism in America is implicitly an attempt by each critic to make of America the kind of country he would like, which in every case is a better country than it is today. . . . As he achieves a sense of values he adopts them, and declares them, and tries to make them prevail."[5] Therefore, when considering Mencken and his contemporaries in 1908, one must realize that one is not dealing with critics engaged in a search for symbols or inspired by a fascination with artistic form. Assuming that literature was the product of culture, they ranged beyond art to consider the society out of which it arose. Mencken's literary criticism, then, should be seen *both* as an attempt to aid the development of a vital, vibrant national literature and as a critique of American society and culture. In Mencken's case, as with most of his fellow critics of the time, the two tasks were deemed inseparable.

Mencken's criticism, particularly prior to 1917, reveals a threefold strategy for the improvement of American letters. First, he vigorously attacked and ridiculed those characteristics of American culture that seemed to obstruct the writer in his effort to come to grips with his society. At the same time, he urged American writers not to look to the past for their inspiration. Rather, he wanted them to turn to contemporary Europe for their models of excellence and to contemporary America for their material. Finally, he conducted in the *Smart Set* a kind of school for American novelists by seeking to define both the novel and the role of the writer and by trying to inculcate in novelists the need for a philosophical approach that would most clearly reveal America to Americans.

## I   *Clearing the Ground*

Toward the end of his fifteen year domination of the *Smart Set* book department, Mencken commented, "My business, considering the state of the society in which I find myself, has been principally to clear the ground of mouldering rubbish, to chase away old ghosts, to help set the artist free."[6] Since this meant trying to break the hold of popular conventions in fiction that tended to work against the emergence of a great literature, sentimentality ranked high on Mencken's list of literary taboos. Reviewing William Allen White's *A Certain Rich Man,* in the *Smart Set* in October 1909, Mencken complained that the Kansas editor turned novelist saw human existence as nothing more than "a good excuse for a sentimental orgy." "Sentimentality," Mencken moaned, "is our national weakness, as bigotry is our national vice" (153, 155). As a result, writers all too frequently failed to depict the reality of American life, and shallow optimism was often preferred to penetrating insight. "The purpose of novel writing, as that crime is practiced in the United States, is not to interpret life, but to varnish, veil and perfume life. . ." (January 1911, 163).

Mencken frequently complained that even when a novelist did

attempt a grasp at reality, his story was often spoiled by the American tendency to turn fiction into an exercise in moralistic didacticism. In his first review in the *Smart Set,* in November 1908, Mencken castigated Upton Sinclair, the muckraking novelist, for having allowed *The Moneychangers* to degenerate into an economic and political tract. Sinclair, he complained, had "hopelessly confused the functions of the novelist with those of the crusader. His story, despite its interest and its craftsmanship, is not a moving picture of human passions, . . . but a somewhat florid thesis in sociology, with conclusions that were stale in the days of St. Augustine" (156).

It was one thing to attack an important figure like Sinclair, but Mencken mustered equal enthusiasm for assaults against the confectioners of mawkish best-selling romances. He obviously enjoyed exercising his satiric bludgeon. Nevertheless, there was a certain seriousness behind his decision to devote five long paragraphs of a review to Marjorie Benton Cooke's *Bambi* or half a review to *Innocent* by Marie Corelli. In his last *Smart Set* piece, in December 1923, Mencken fumed, "If a critic has any duty at all, save the primary duty to be true to himself, it is the public duty of protecting the fine arts against the invasion of such frauds. They are insidious in their approach; they know how to cajole and deceive; unchallenged, they are apt to bag many victims. Once they are permitted to get a foothold, however insecure, it becomes doubly hard to combat them. My method, therefore, has been to tackle them at first sight and with an ax" (143).

## II  *Europe and America*

Although much of Mencken's criticism was devoted to trying to eradicate the bad and the banal from American fiction, it would be a mistake to regard him as a negative force. While trying to pinpoint the factors in American literature and culture that hampered good writing, Mencken also sought to keep his readers abreast of the best material coming from England, Ireland, and the Continent. If, as he thought, models for excellence were lacking at home, then they had to be sought for abroad. In suggesting this turn toward Europe, Mencken was urging upon his *Smart Set* readers the pattern of his own self-directed education. With almost the single exception of Mark Twain, Mencken had found his inspiration in such European figures as Hardy, Conrad, Shaw, Ibsen, and Nietzsche; and

Mencken continued this transatlantic focus after he joined the *Smart Set*. He became one of the first and certainly most enthusiastic champions of Joseph Conrad in America, he maintained a constant flow of reviews of European authors, and, for a time, few important figures in the British Isles or on the Continent failed to catch his eye.

Mencken's European outlook did create one perplexing problem, however. He did not accept the assumption of many within the Genteel Tradition that American writing was and would remain a province of English literature. Yet, in trying to make Americans aware of the innovations and the quality of European authors, he ran the double danger of either urging American writers to imitate Europeans or inferring that American culture was inimical to art. He certainly came close to embracing this last pessimistic conclusion. For a long while he tended to define as European or foreign those qualities he admired in his favorite American writers and critics. In *A Book of Prefaces* (1917) he depicted his mentor, James Huneker, as a lonely figure in American criticism, "as exotic as a samovar, as essentially un-American as a bashibazouk, a nose ring or a fugue" (187). In praising Theodore Dreiser's *Jennie Gerhardt*, Mencken found the novel "so European in its method, its point of view, its almost reverential seriousness, that one can scarcely imagine an American writing it."[7]

Although Mencken never clearly defined this "European" point of view, he did call attention in his *Prefaces* to "that 'obscure inner necessity' of which Conrad tells us, that irresistable creative passion of a genuine artist, standing spellbound before the impenetrable enigma that is life . . . challenged by a wondering and half-terrified sort of representation of what passes understanding" (147). By adopting this philosophical attitude, Mencken believed that American writers could rise above sentimentality and optimism to present a more complex, challenging, and disturbing view of life.

Although Mencken frequently despaired of the state of American literature, he never consciously called upon native writers to imitate European material or even styles. Nothing infuriated him more than what he called the "absurd fear of nationalism" in American arts. Americans, he believed, could learn from Europe, but they had to write about their own country and use their own voices. As a critic, then, Mencken was a nationalist. When commenting on contemporary music in 1909, he noted that "An American trying to write like a

German is essentially an absurdity. But an American trying to write as an American might conceivably thrill the world. . . ."[8] Like Van Wyck Brooks and Randolph Bourne, Mencken was engaged in what Morton D. Zabel has called the "Americanization" of the arts.

Therefore, when the English drama critic William Archer complained that American playwrights had made little progress in their craft, Mencken admitted that his country had not yet produced a Shaw or a Pinero. Nevertheless, he believed that progress would be made. "Around the corner the first really great American play may be waiting. Let us assume that it is and so prepare ourselves to receive and recognize it."[9] For this reason, Mencken frequently withheld his satiric invective when he came across a young American writer whose flawed work nevertheless showed promise. "I read novel after novel without encountering a single idea," he wrote in the *Smart Set* in January 1911. "Therefore, when I happen upon one that is full of ideas, I rejoice and am exceedingly glad, and shout the news at the top of my voice" (164).

On the other hand, Mencken considered established and respectable literary figures fair game. One of his favorite targets was no less a person than William Dean Howells, "the dean" of American criticism. In spite of the fact that Howells had played an important role in furthering the cause of American Realism, Mencken criticized him for his alleged "paralyzing surrender to Boston notions of what is nice" and for having surrounded Mark Twain with a "pink fog" of gentility. Henry James also came under fire. James, Mencken felt, had made the grave mistake of leaving America for London. The expatriate would have done better had he gone west to Chicago, where he would have been "vastly improved by a few wiffs from the . . . stupendous abattoirs."[10]

All of this negative criticism was a part of Mencken's strategy as a critic. Just as he felt that contemporary European literature could be used as a model and inspiration for American writers, he was equally adamant that the established figures of the previous generation of American writers had become obstacles in the paths of young and nonconforming authors. Thus he suggested, perhaps none too wisely, that American novelists would learn much more from Sherwood Anderson's *Winesburg, Ohio* than they would from Howells and James.[11] In this way Mencken's reviews rapidly took on the aspect of a symbolic battlefield where European excellence was arrayed against American mediocrity, the young literary rebels against the old respectability, the unpopular and dissenting voice against conventional sentimentality and moralism. By thus personalizing criticism, he gave the younger generation of writers literary heroes and villians who were to stir their imaginations. A simplistic and often misleading approach, it was instrumental in polarizing the literary attitudes during the decade from 1910 to 1920. Moreover, it did help to create a critical environment in which the cultural tensions of the nation were thrown into stark, if not always accurate, relief.

This tendency to play off Europe against America, or the new against the old, temporarily obscured for Mencken the need to discover or create a viable national cultural tradition upon which young writers could build. He was largely unmoved by Van Wyck Brooks's call for a "usable past." Because Mencken's own usable past lay in his special and idiosyncratic reading in the European tradition of cultural iconoclasm from Voltaire through Huxley to Shaw, he felt no need to seek out native precursors. In fact, whenever he referred to American nineteenth century writers of stature, such as Walt Whitman or Edgar Allen Poe, Mencken usually depicted them as standing quite outside of the mainstream of American literature. They were, in his opinion, isolated figures in a cultural landscape in which they could find no meaningful place, and, as a result, they were misunderstood and rejected by their society.

### III   *The Romantic Realist*

One of the factors that entitled Mencken to the status of a literary critic, as opposed to a mere reviewer of books, was his continuing, conscious attempt to instruct both his readers and the younger generation of writers in those qualities necessary for a good novel. While his ideas were not especially original, they were usually esthetically sound and, given the uncertain state of American criticism and writing in the prewar years and in the early 1920s, they were important. Reviewing one of Gertrude Atherton's novels in September 1912, Mencken voiced one of his major complaints. The author had, he asserted, "neglected the first business of a serious novelist, which is to interpret and account for her characters, to criticize life as well as to describe it . . ." (153). The novelist's task involved more than inventiveness and style: he or she needed an intellectual and philosophical point of view. A novel had to "make comprehensible the philosophy of life of a whole community or race of men by showing us how the philosophy accords with the impulses and satisfies the yearnings of typical individuals."[12]

Although Mencken refused to be dogmatic about points of criticism, he did make it clear that the philosophy of life that, in his opinion, produced the most superior fiction was the one that recognized the essential meaninglessness of life. In *A Book of Prefaces* he stated that "human life is a seeking without a finding, that its purpose is impenetrable, that joy and sorrow are alike meaningless . . ." (15). In his review of Dreiser's *Jennie Gerhardt*, Mencken noted with approval "the same profound pessimism which gives a dark color to the best that we have from Hardy, Moore, Zola and the great Russians—the pessimism of disillusion . . . that pessimism which comes with the discovery that the riddle of life . . . is essentially insoluble" (November 1911, 155). Translating this view into the demands of fiction, Mencken claimed that "The aim of a genuine novel is not merely to decribe a particular man, but to describe a typical man, and to show him in active conflict with a more or less permanent and recognizable environment—fighting it, taking color from it, succumbing to it" (June 1914, 153).

Although these statements have a distinct suggestion of Naturalism about them, Mencken never applied that term to novels that he admired. In fact, he was generally critical of the school of European Naturalists, as when, for instance, he decried the "flea-hunting naturalism" of Zola and his followers. What was left out of their "scientific pornographies," he complained was the "realism" that stressed the "failure of society to fit into an orderly scheme of causes and effects, virtues and rewards, crimes and punishments. What [Naturalism] leaves out is the glow of romance that hangs about that failure—the poignant drama of bland chance, the fascination of the unknowable." The Naturalists were bad artists, Mencken concluded, because they did not appreciate beauty.[13]

What Mencken wanted the artist to depict was not so much the Naturalist's vision of man as a mere pawn, as the helpless victim of a deterministic universe, but rather man's doomed rebellion against that universe—what he called the "eternal struggle between man's will and his destiny" (February 1910, 158). There is a distinctly Romantic quality, absent in European Naturalism, in Mencken's insistence that all great fiction concerned "one man's struggle against fate." Praising Frank Norris's *Vandover and the Brute* in August 1914, Mencken agreed with the author's estimation of him-

self that he was "something of a romanticist . . . as every great
realist always is . . ." (158). Concerning Dreiser, Mencken denied
that the novelist was either a Naturalist or a Realist. In *Prefaces*,
Mencken noted: "He is really something quite different, and in his
moments, something far more stately. His aim is not merely to
record, but to translate and understand; the thing he exposes is not
the empty event and act, but the endless mystery out of which it
springs; his pictures have a passionate compassion in them that it is
hard to separate from poetry" (136).

Mencken rejected the Naturalist's belief that art could be an objective, scientific representation of life; and, like all Realists,
Mencken believed that art involved the selection and ordering of
reality. "Art can never by simple representation," he noted in *Prejudices: First Series* (1919). "It must, at least, present the real in the
light of some recognizable ideal; it must give to the eternal farce, if
not some moral, then at all events some direction"(44). Mencken
the critic was a Realist. However, like Norris and, indeed, Dreiser,
he was also something of a Romantic. His search for those qualities
of the "endless mystery" of life and the "passionate compassion" in
the handling of characters inspired the best moments in Mencken's
criticism.

Apart from Mencken's commitment to the style of Realism and his
sound but very general ideas about the proper philosophical approach to fiction, it cannot be said that Mencken's prewar criticism
reveals any comprehensive theory of the novel. In fact, he had
difficulty deciding whether the main emphasis in a work should lie
with the characters or with their background and environment.
After World War I, however, Mencken tried to pull his ideas together and did offer a very narrow concept of the form and function
of the novel. In one of his last pieces of criticism, published in
*Prejudices: Fifth Series* (1926), Mencken insisted that the good novel
is always "a character sketch of an individual not far removed from
the norm of the race" (219). In the best contemporary American
novels, he claimed, it was not the storyline or the ideas that stood
out, but the characters. He felt this emphasis was proper, for he
believed that American society had produced more lively and di-
verting character types than all other nations taken together. Therefore, he urged American novelists to depict the "particular richness
of the American scene in sharply outlined and racy characters"
(220).

This emphasis on character types moved Mencken closer to a sociological view of the novel. It is significant that among his favorite authors of the 1920s were Ring Lardner and Sinclair Lewis. However, while Mencken was urging Lardner, Lewis, and even F. Scott Fitzgerald to immortalize the moralists and evangelists, the politicians, and the confidence men who peopled the American scene, Mencken never lost sight, as some of his admirers occasionally did, of the need to keep the Romantic element in focus. For him the great gap between aspiration and attainment was the most dramatic and poignant element in American life.

Thus Mencken's main criticism of Ring Lardner, a writer whom he greatly admired, was that the author was only amused by his characters and did not pity them in their stupidity. In *Prejudices: Fifth Series,* Mencken suggested, "The moron, perhaps, has a place in fiction, as in life, but he is not to be treated too easily and casually. It must be shown that he suffers tragically because he cannot abandon the plow to write poetry, or the sample-case to study opera" (38). Again, in the same vein, he added a warning to his advice that writers would find a rich subject in the American moral reformer. Such a character type, he noted in the same volume of *Prejudices,* had to be seen as one "eternally in the position of a man trying to empty the ocean with a tin-dipper. He will be mauled, and the chance he offers thrown away, if the novelist who attempts him in the end forgets the tragedy under his comedy. . . . A novelist blind to that capital fact will never comprehend the type. It needs irony—but above all it needs pity" (232).

This concept of irony and pity became not only the major theme of Mencken's criticism in the early 1920s but also an esthetic counterbalance to the kind of sociological and satirical fiction that he himself, both as a critic and as an editor, was helping to promote. That he made the point so obviously and often suggests that he may have feared that, with the passing of the Genteel Tradition with its idealism and its sentimentality, the younger writers were swinging to the other extreme and were depicting life as nothing but a shallow farce. Indeed, Mencken is still often accused of having fathered an easy cynicism among the younger writers of thie postwar years; but no other critic worked harder than he did in order to maintain a balance between satire and sympathetic understanding. In his *Prejudices: First Series,* he took the English author Arnold Bennett to task for depicting his characters as only "mean figures in an infinitely dispersed and unintelligible farce, as hopeless nobodies in an epic struggle that transcends both their volition and their comprehension." The reader thus missed "the responsive recognition, the sympathy of poor mortal soul for poor mortal soul, the tidal uprush of feeling that makes us all one" (38).

## IV  *A Critic Is a Critic Is a Critic*

Although Mencken did manage to come to some conclusions about the novel, his various attempts to define criticism and his own place as a critic tended to change with the ever-shifting focus of his interests. For the most part Mencken distrusted labels and categories, and he did his best to squirm out from under them when he could. Thus he claimed in his "Autobiographical Notes," which he put together in 1925, "I am simply an eclectic" (173). Certainly Mencken's tastes were broad. At one time or another he championed such dissimilar writers as Conrad, H. G. Wells, Bennett, Dreiser, Sinclair Lewis, Fitzgerald, and James Branch Cabell. Usually he tried to spread the blanket of Realism over as many of his favorites as he could. He even claimed Cabell (whose imaginary medieval kingdom of Poictesme might seem as far from Realism as any American writer might choose to wander) as a Realist in spirit, if not in style. "Realism is simply intellectual honesty in the artist. . . . He makes no compromises with popular sentimentality and illusion. He avoids the false inference as well as the bogus fact. He respects his material as he respects himself."[14]

Mencken shied away from pinning down his own critical position, partly because he placed the freedom of the artist above everything, including his own critical dictums. In his "Autobiographical Notes" he claimed, "The test, to me, is not the man's programme, but his honesty. If he is making a sincere effort to do something worth while I am disposed to allow him a wide latitude in the choice of the means. This attitude, I find, is incomprehensible to many persons. They cannot grasp the concept of liberty" (173). Admittedly, even Mencken sometimes lost sight of this concept when he read works that lay outside of the limits of his own tastes and comprehension. Thus he frequently took the expatriate writers of the 1920s to task for having abandoned the fecund material of their native heath in order to carry out surrealistic experiments in the garrets of Europe. His attitude toward poetry, while not as uninformed as his critics have contended, made him totally unresponsive to such complex writers as Robert Frost and T. S. Elliot.[15]

On the whole, however, Mencken's concern for the freedom of the artist was genuine. It was this concern for artistic freedom that attracted him initially to Joel Spingarn's influential book *Creative Criticism* (1917). Spingarn, in a chapter entitled "The New Criticism" held that the critic's first and foremost duty was to discover what the artist's intentions were in a given work. Mencken agreed with Spingarn's basic premise: that the author's work should be judged, not in terms of preexisting theories or ideologies, but in terms of itself. However, in his essay "Criticism of Criticism of Criticism," in *Prejudices: First Series*, Mencken issued an early warning against carrying the New Criticism too far. "[B]eauty as we know it in this world is by no means the apparition *in vacuo* that Dr. Spingarn seems to see. It has its social, its political, even its moral implications." "Brahms," Mencken noted, "wrote his Deutsches Requiem, not only because he was a great artist, but also because he was a good German" (18). It is ironic that while Mencken was one of the first critics to help popularize Springarn's theories, his own reputation was almost totally eclipsed in the 1930s and 1940s as the New Criticism became the new orthodoxy among American academic critics.[16]

The critic, like the artist, must be seen within the context of his times. Few American critics prior to the mid-1920s were deeply involved with those problems of form and symbolism that were to become the focal points for so much American criticism in the following decades. Mencken's generation took it for granted that the cultural and social implications of a work of art were as important as its form or technique. What was needed in those years were critics who would help spread ideas, who would champion the new and the unpopular, who would fight for the right of the artist to express himself in his own way, and who would turn American writers toward the material within their own society. These were Mencken's goals as a critic, and it was his pursuit of these goals that made him a major critical force in those years.

As a critic, Mencken unquestionably had his limitations. His ideas, while often sound in themselves, were neither brilliant nor original. He made no real contributions to the theories of literature or criticism. He had many blind spots. He was totally unaffected by the revolution in writing created by such figures as Ezra Pound, T. S. Elliot, William Butler Yeats, and James Joyce. As Burton Rascoe, a fellow critic who was one of Mencken's first champions, noted in 1922: "The truth is that the literary generation now gaining recognition has progressed beyond the reaches of Mencken's aesthetic equipment."[17] Within his limitations, however, Mencken's power as a critic lay in his almost intuitive understanding of good writing and in his deep empathy for writers. One still turns to his commentaries on Conrad, Lardner, George Ade, Sinclair Lewis, Cabell, and Fitzgerald for both pleasure and enlightenment. His essays on Dreiser remain unsurpassed for their sympathy and insight. Finally, more than any other critic of the period, Mencken had the ability to make people interested—to get them involved—in the problems facing American literature.

### CHAPTER 4

# Social Criticism in Prewar America, 1910–1915

## I  The Free Lance

BY 1906, Mencken, who was then twenty-five years old, had become the managing editor of the Baltimore *Herald* and the secretary to the paper's board of directors. On June 11 of that year the *Herald* collapsed, and Mencken had to find himself a new employer. His sense of responsiblity toward his widowed mother and his attachment to Baltimore ruled out any move to the more important centers for journalism, such as Chicago or New York. After a brief month on the Baltimore *Evening News,* Mencken joined the staff of the city's *Sunpapers* in July 1906, and so began a connection that he would maintain for most of the remainder of his career. As the editor of the Sunday edition and then, in 1910, as the editor of the *Evening Sun,* Mencken began to attract attention. In 1911, his editorials for the *Evening Sun* (signed "H. L. M.") caught the eye of one of the paper's owners, who suggested that Mencken be given his own daily, signed column and a totally free hand to write about whatever he wished. The result was the "Free Lance," which Mencken himself described as a "private editorial column devoted wholly to my personal opinions and prejudices."[1]

The "Free Lance" began on May 9, 1911. Mencken's iconoclasm soon generated so much reaction that many protesting letters began to arrive at the *Sun*'s office. Consistent with his love of controversy, Mencken asked for and received control of a column next to his own in which he printed the most vigorous of the attacks against him. "This was partly mere bombast and braggadocia," he later recalled, "but also partly genuine belief in free speech."[2]

Mencken's opinions about politics and society were by now an amalgam of his Social Darwinism, his Nietzscheanism, and his dedication to the idea of an iconoclastic elite. In 1910, he and Socialist editor R. R. La Monte published a dialogue entitled *Men Versus the Man* which contains the rudiments of Mencken's social philosophy. Essentially, Mencken recognized only one single division within society: the superior individual against the inferior mob.

In one of his contributions to *Men Versus the Man* Mencken maintained that the prime quality of the superior man was "a sort of restless impatience with things as they are—a sort of insatiable desire to help along the evolutionary process" (113). Because the inferior man lacked these virtues, he deserved the place to which nature had assigned him—the bottom of the heap. "He is forever down-trodden and oppressed. He is forever opposed to a surrender of his immemorial superstitions, prejudices, swinishness, and inertia. He is forever certain that, if only some god would lend him a hand and give him his just rights, he would be rich, happy and care-free. And he is forever and utterly wrong" (112). Therefore, any political system based on the participation of the masses was doomed by its false doctrine that a man, "merely by virtue of being a man, is fitted to take a hand in the adjudication of all the world's most solemn and difficult causes" (151).

Although highly critical of democracy in 1910, Mencken had not yet begun to associate the worst aspects of democracy with the American system. The United States fell short of its democratic ideals, Mencken noted in *Men Versus the Man*, and rightly so. "Once a year, we reaffirm the doctrine that all men are free and equal. All the rest of the twelvemonth we devote our energies to proving that they are not" (152). Should a real democracy be actually instituted, Mencken insisted, "There would be an end to all progress. Emotion would take the place of reason. It would be impossible to achieve coherent governmental policies" (153).

This concern for rational progress was a counterbalance to Mencken's suspicion of democracy. It made him, in spite of himself, a constructive critic of government. During the early days of the "Free Lance," his main target was corrupt and inefficient government led by self-serving politicians who played upon the stupidity of the masses. Good government, on the other hand, was efficient, honest, enlightened, and *active;* it iconoclastically cut away the old, fradulent pieties of special privileges and emotional party ties in order to run society along intelligent, modern lines. While Mencken clearly rejected Bryanesque liberalism, which equated better government with increased democracy, he did not cling to the old-fashioned laissez-faire attitudes. Like many others during the Progressive years, Mencken was trying to find a new direction in American politics.

For example, he championed the idea of a strong executive over what he considered venal and stodgy representative institutions. Along with many urban reformers, he called for a great reduction in the powers of rural-dominated state legislatures over the cities. In urban "home rule" he saw the first essential step toward improving city government; but Mencken even went so far as to argue that state legislatures and city councils should be stripped of their powers. They were the "headquarters of all governmental incompetence, stupidity and corruptions." "What state," he asked in his *Sun* column of May 22, 1911, "will be the first to abolish its legislature?" In place of representative bodies, Mencken advocated the strong use of executive power by mayors, city managers, governors, and even presidents. In 1911 he welcomed the election of reform governor Woodrow Wilson in New Jersey; for, with the people behind a strong leader, "not even a dubious legislature can affront or defy him."[3]

It is significant that Mencken's real political hero was Theodore Roosevelt. Commenting on Roosevelt's European trip in 1910, Mencken suggested that Europeans saw the ex-president as "a visible symbol of all the great qualities which enter into the spirit of Americanism. They regard him . . . as the archtype of the energetic, resourceful, idol-smashing American. . . ." Roosevelt was the spokesman of American efficiency, and this spirit was "the one thing that sets the United States apart from all other nations. We are sworn foes to formalism in all departments of thought and life. Our one god is progress—and Colonel Roosevelt is the high priest in the temple."[4] Mencken, like his hero, felt that efficient and dynamic leadership should involve itself with the introduction of modernizing reforms for society as well as for politics. Public health was one of the principle areas that Mencken saw in need of such leadership. A well-informed layman on medical matters and acquainted with some of Baltimore's more advanced doctors, Mencken used his "Free Lance" column to campaign for an improvement in the city's dismal record on malaria and typhoid. Typically, he blamed the problem on the backwardness of the people and on the fears of timorous politicians about bringing in unpopular and vigorous reforms.

When local politicians and civic boosters complained that Mencken's publicizing of Baltimore's health problems was hurting the city's image, the "Free Lance" lashed out in January 3, 1913, at those who seemed to believe "that every raid upon established custom, and particularly upon established hoggishness, hurts business, and that no city can survive such damage. Their ideal is commercial prosperity, and they are determined to get it if half of humanity must _rot for it." Although an unrepentent supporter of capitalism, Mencken was far from enamored with the progress of industrialism in his city—nor did he admire the values upon which it seemed to thrive. "The time will come, no doubt, when a man who proposes to put 500 women to work in a factory at four dollars a week will be sent to jail as an enemy to society, instead of being fawned upon as a public benefactor, as at present. . . . We still estimate all such enterprises by the money they produce and not, as we should, by the human beings they produce" (June 23, 1911).[5]

The value of Mencken's iconoclasm was that he could cut across ideological boundaries in an unideological way. The same was true of his treatment of racial barriers; for although not a liberal on racial matters, Mencken did ask Baltimoreans to consider both the justice and the wisdom of the growing policy of housing segregation, which forced blacks, no matter what their status, to remain in unhealthy slums, the breeding grounds for typhoid and tuberculosis. Other areas of reform also interested the "Free Lance." Mencken vehemently attacked capital punishment. He gave cautious approval to the "Oregan Plan"—the initiative, referendum, and recall. He supported the direct primary and even the new state of Arizona's proposal for the recall of judges. "The one way to prove the good or evil of new schemes of government is to test them in practice. And the best place to test them is in the new states, where the insecurity and fluency of institutions are taken for granted and comparatively little harm can be done by sudden change."[6]

This tolerance for experimentation was a part of the general reform atmosphere of Progressivism. Some of Mencken's ideas, however, clearly ran counter to the main stream of reformist thought. He continued to war against the dangers of democracy, claiming in one "Free Lance" article that "Universal manhood suffrage is the cancer that eats at the vitals of the republic. No improvement will ever be real until that cancer is cut out" (July 23, 1912). The great masses of people, he contended, "are against all those varieties of change which involve risk and sacrifice. . . . Their proper function is to execute the ideas of their betters. It is highly dangerous to let them manufacture ideas themselves" (June 5, 1913). Those who were too ignorant to mark their ballot slips properly should not be disqualified in an election but permanently disfranchised.

Even here, however, in this return to the attitudes of the old school of tie-wig Federalism, Mencken also managed to be more "progressive" than many dedicated democratic-minded reformers. He condemned the various attempts at legal disfranchisement of Maryland blacks as totally dishonorable. He also supported women's suffrage, although not on the usually idealistic grounds that women voters would somehow purify politics. He saw it as simply a matter of justice that women, particularly working girls who suffered under the "double slavery" of brute marriage and industrialism, should have a right to help frame the laws that affected their welfare. He was thus opposed to arbitrary restriction of the franchise by race or sex. "A black Lincoln would be just as much a Lincoln as Abe himself, and a Pasteur in skirts would still be worth hearing and heeding," he insisted on June 5, 1913. "Before we may begin to edit and denaturize democracy, we must first give democracy a fair trial, and it has not yet had that fair trial." In the end, however, Mencken remained convinced that society would eventually be forced to consider the franchise not as a right but as "a thing the citizen must earn by his ability and his industry. . . ."

Mencken's attitudes during the Progressive period seem so idiosyncratic, so lacking in either liberal or conservative consistency, that it is tempting to consider him a complete maverick. Yet the fact remains that Mencken did support many of the reforms dear to the hearts of urban Progressives—clean government, executive leadership, administrative efficiency, political experimentation, urban home rule, civic improvements, public health. Mencken's support for such reforms based on modernization and efficiency marks him as a Progressive, but his suspicion of democracy places him within the conservative end of the Progressive spectrum.

The idea of a conservative Progressive might seem a contridiction in terms only if one follows the tradition in American historiography that assumes all reform to be the product of liberal movements.

Bismarck's Germany and the Britain of Benjamin Disraeli and Arthur Balfour show that in other countries reform can sometimes be a conservative phenomenon. While it may be argued that the liberal elements predominated in America during the Progressive period, Progressivism was by no means a monolithic force. It was so diverse in terms of people and ideas that it is better described as a mood rather than as a movement.[7] Some of the reform theories that came out of it were in actual conflict with one another. William Jennings Bryan's demands for more direct democracy were very different in spirit from the Rooseveltian approach to reform, which placed its faith in decisions made by experts and technicians.

In this light, Mencken's support for Roosevelt, an avowed Progressive, has added significance. Mencken saw Roosevelt as an American Nietzsche who, despite the fact that he played fast and loose with public emotions, still had "great foresight and sagacity." "He is not an orthodox man, true enough, but he is at least a man who supports his reasoning intelligently, and shows intellectual hospitality and alertness." He would be dangerous, Mencken concluded on June 11, 1912, in a "Free Lance" article, if Roosevelt believed his own democratic "balderdash," but "what reflective man accuses him of believing it?" Even in the 1920s Mencken remained convinced that Roosevelt's heart had never been moved by Bryanism or Wilsonian democratic liberalism. Writing in *Prejudices: Second Series* (1920), Mencken observed:

Roosevelt, for all his fluent mastery of democratic counter-words, democratic gestures and all the rest of the armamentarium of the mob-master, had no such faith in his heart of hearts. He didn't believe in democracy; he believed simply in government. His remedy for all the great pangs and longings of existence was not a dispersion of authority, but a hard concentration of authority. He was not in favor of unlimited experiment; he was in favor of a rigid control from above, a despotism of inspired prophets and policemen. He was not for democracy as his followers understood democracy, and as it actually is and must be; he was for a paternalism of the true Bismarkian pattern . . . a paternalism concerning itself with all things. . . . His instincts were always those of the property-owning Tory, not those of the romantic Liberal. (123–24)

By this time Mencken himself had ceased to be enamored by centralization or paternalism in government; but he still admired Roosevelt for what he took to be the president's originality in trying to find a dynamic but nondemocratic approach to reform. Although the accuracy of his interpretation of Roosevelt may be debated, the important thing is that this view helps clarify Mencken's position regarding Progressivism. When he voted for Roosevelt in 1912, he thought he was voting for a reform leader who was operating from an essentially conservative basis. [8]

Woodrow Wilson defeated Roosevelt in 1912; and, as the liberalism of the New Freedom waxed, Mencken's interest in reform began to wane. Mencken himself had never embraced the term "Progressivism"; and, in spite of Roosevelt's attempt to use the term, Mencken continued to apply the word to the democratic side of the reform mood. As early as July 23, 1912, he quipped in the "Free Lance" that "A progressive is one who believes that the common people are both intelligent and honest; a reactionary is one who knows better." By June 20, 1914, he was so disgruntled with the turn that reform had taken that he issued a manifesto of reaction. "Up with the black flag! The time has come for honest men to throw off all disguises. The uplift has failed in politics as it has in morals. The country has been made ridiculous abroad and darn near ruined at home. . . . Down with direct elections! Down with muckraking! Down with the new freedom! . . . Down with mob rule! . . . Down with bogus progressivism! . . . Up with Civilization! . . . The people are ripe for rescue."

Mencken was reacting to more than Wilsonian liberalism. His reference to the "uplift," a popular term for moral reform during the Progressive Era, suggests that he felt that Progressivism had saddled the country with something more than an excess of political democracy. It had created, in his view, a militant, intolerant, moralistic spirit that invaded the privacy and threatened the sanctity of the individual.

## II  *Crusade Against Crusades*

The pressure for moral reform, which accompanied the movement for political and social reform after 1900, is one of the most startling cultural phenomena of the Progressive period. As historian Clyde Griffen has observed, "The progressives grew up with a moral consensus so clear and unquestioned that they tended to assume this consensus was characteristic of human nature whenever it was permitted to develop freely. This assumption easily fostered righteous indignation against violators of the consensus; personalities with an authoritarian warp carried this to the blind intolerance of 'sinners' which not infrequently appears in progressive crusades against intemperance, gambling, and prostitution."[9] With industrialization, urbanization, and immigration, the old rural Protestant values that had been the core of this moral consensus were coming under increasing pressure. The moral reformers within the Progressive ranks were driven not only by their faith in their values but also by an aggressive attempt to meet the challenge of urban secularization and cultural pluralism.

Mencken's Baltimore experienced its share of this conflict. Protestant evangelists, Anti-Saloon Leaguers, and vice crusaders preached the necessity for proscriptive legislation as a cure for social ills. Using the "Free Lance" as his platform, Mencken sought to organize local resistance against these drives for moral legislation. Under the banner of libertarianism, Mencken waged a crusade against the moral crusaders. Attempts at censoring books or the theater drew from him the accusation that such laws were "revolutionary and dangerous" and could turn the policeman into "the most lawless man among us." Angered at efforts to curtail secular entertainments on Sundays, Mencken complained on June 1, 1911, that "Virtue, once it grows militant and tyrannical, tends to become a vice." It also tended to be self-defeating. Mencken pointed out that when vice crusaders attempted to destroy the old "red light" district they often simply spread prostitution throughout the city "Nothing has ever been accomplished in Christiandom," he warned on November 7, 1912, "by proceeding upon the theory that sin is a purely volitional phenomenon, to be stamped out by invective. All the moral progress we have made has been based upon frank acceptance of human frailty, and common-sense endeavor to diminish the evil in its inevitable effects." Mencken's most vitriolic attacks, however, were reserved for the growing movement for the prohibition of alcohol, a subject discussed later in the context of the 1920s.

Mencken's opposition to the moral crusade was essentially libertarian, because behind each particular threat to convenience or personal taste that was posed by moralistic legislation, he always saw a greater danger to liberty. On January 11, 1913, he accused the militant moralists of trying to "steal liberty and self-respect, and the man who has lost both is a man who has lost everything that separates a civilized freeman from a convict in a chain gang." Indeed, Mencken went so far as to urge Baltimoreans to defy all proscriptive legislation when and where it was possible. Charles Bonaparte, a former member of Theodore Roosevelt's administration and the leader of the Baltimore Reform League, informed the "Free Lance" that a citizen was duty bound to obey all laws as long as they remained on the books. In response, Mencken insisted on January 8, 1913, that laws that invaded the citizen's rights and privacy were beyond the pale of obedience. In such a case, the citizen "is bound to resist such laws to the full extent of his courage and ingenuity, so long as the chances of success remain in his favor. . . .In brief, the decent citizen has to protect himself against legislative snouting and tyranny, for it is only by protecting himself that he can protect civilization. The law, when it falls into the hands of moral maniacs, becomes itself a desperate criminal."

Mencken regarded the drive for social control through moralistic legislation as a real threat to individualism and to traditional American liberty. Rightly or wrongly, he also came to see the moral crusade as an extension of Progressive reform, which, in his mind, had drifted from a rational leadership from above into the hands of democratic emotionalism from below. For this reason, Mencken turned so vehemently against Progressivism that he conveniently ignored the fact that he himself had partaken of the Progressive mood and had supported many Progressive reforms.

### III  *"The American": 1913*

This change in Mencken's attitude toward reform between 1912 and 1913 was part of his general shift in his attitude toward his country. Although increasingly critical of many aspects of American culture and society, Mencken had continued to criticize his country from the inside: that is, he adopted the persona of the bemused but concerned citizen who found his society violating its own value system. By 1913, this persona underwent a simple but dramatic change; for Mencken suddenly appeared to be criticizing America from the outside and to be using a value system that, he implied, was not a part of his society but exterior and superior to it. In terms of style, he accomplished this change by a simple alteration in the possessive pronouns used when writing about America and Americans. Where he had previously written about "we" Americans and "our" problems, he now used the terms "the" American and "his" problems. As a result, Mencken suggested a sweeping indictment against all things American.

Several factors contributed to the hardening of Mencken's critical attitude toward his country: his struggle to improve American literature in the face of mediocrity and cultural conservatism; his disillusionment with reform; and his concern about militant moralism. Another factor was his trip to Europe in the spring of 1912, when he first came into direct contact with societies and cultures that offered a dramatic contrast to his own. For the first part of the trip he was just one more Yankee tourist who was making the obligatory rounds of Gibraltar, Rome, Paris, and London. When he arrived in Germany, the land of his forebearers, Mencken's ideal of the superior society suddenly materialized before him. There he thought he had discovered a land of beauty, tradition, and order that had, at the same time, a powerful sense of modern efficiency[10]

Within a year after his return from Europe, Mencken began for the *Smart Set* a series of articles about American society and the national character. The articles were intended to be the basis for a book. That book was never published, but the articles mark Mencken's most ambitious attempt thus far at satiric criticism. The six articles in the series ran intermittently from June 1913 to February 1914. After an introductory essay that bore the title of the series, "The American," other pieces were subtitled "His Morals," "His Language," "His Freedom," and "His New Puritanism."[11]

The effectiveness of Mencken's satire in this series was based on two innovations. One, already noted, was the adoption of the persona of the outsider; the other was the constant inversion of the myths that Americans cherished about themselves. For example, Mencken took the myth of American individualism and converted it into an image of American conformity. In perhaps no other country in the world, he claimed in October 1913, was any deviation from the accepted norm met with such "utter social and political extinction" as in the United States. In his view the American was "so little the soul-free individualist that it is almost impossible for him to imagine himself save as a member of a crowd. All of his thinking is done, and most of his acts are done, not as a free individual, but as one of a muddled mass of individuals. . . .He does not stand for something; he belongs to something" (85). Carrying out a similar inversion of the myth about American liberty, Mencken declared that "there is probably no civilized man who knows less of genuine liberty, either personal or political, than the American." To Mencken, the Yankee was surrounded by so many prohibitions concerning his morals that "it has become almost impossible for a citizen . . . to get through a day without violating at least one of them. . . . In every relation of life the private conduct of the American is minutely regulated" (82).

Mencken also denied his countryman's proud belief that his government was the most advanced in the world. Americans, he wrote in June 1913, enjoyed opportunity to change old platitudes for new ones. "But certainly not opportunity to tackle head on and with a surgeon's courage the greater and graver problems of being and becoming, to draw a sword upon the time worn and doddering delusions of the race, to clear away the corruptions that make government a game for thieves and morals a petty vice for old-maids and patriotism a last refuge of scoundrels. . ." (94). Instead of freeing the individual, Mencken insisted in October 1913, that American democracy placed the citizen under the tyranny of the majority. "A democracy made up of assertive individualists, each reacting upon all the others, would be a democracy extremely jealous of human rights and extremely sensitive to new ideas." In the United States, however, democracy consisted of the maneuverings of two major political parties that were "two disorderly mobs, each wholly careless of the rights of the other" and each "highly resistant to purely intelligent suggestion" (86).

The American who emerged from Mencken's articles was a far cry from the national myth of the courageous, self-reliant individualist. In the new Menckenized version, he became a figure haunted by fears; fears of the minority groups below him, of the powerful and wealthy above him, of the beauty he could not appreciate, and of the new and different ideas that disturbed him. Primarily, however, Mencken's American of October 1913, was afraid of *himself*. "His dominant passion is not for self-expression, but for self-effacement. He performs the function of a citizen, not as a free ego, but as a mere cipher, a nameless soldier in a large army" (87).

Mencken blamed the cause of this failure of spirit on Puritanism, or rather the "New Puritanism," as the title of his final article in February 1914, suggested. According to Mencken, the Puritanism of seventeenth century New England had been an introspective concern for the individual's spiritual well-being and had been based upon renunciation and asceticism. Modern Puritanism, however, was aggressive; and it sought to dominate society not with spiritual ideals but with moral coersion. Puritanism had become a debased form of Nietzsche's "Will to Power," "a wild scramble into Heaven on the backs of harlots" (89). The primary reason for this change in American Puritanism was, according to Mencken, the result of the accumulation of industrial wealth that followed the Civil War. "In brief, puritanism has become militant by becoming rich" (89). As a result of this "trustification" of religion, the Puritan could "combat immorality with the weapons designed for crime" (91). Imposed upon an undisciplined democracy, Puritanism, by means of "uplift" or moral reform, had made its assault on culture, order, and individual liberty.

Although Mencken's attempt to combine Nietzschean psychology with an economic interpretation of Puritanism is not without interest, he clearly had only a superficial grasp of American religious history. Those characteristics that Mencken apparently believed to be Puritan—sentimental evangelical piety, bourgeois moralism, the business ethic, excessive reforming zeal—had little or nothing to do with Puritanism as a historical force. Mencken was not alone, of course, in this distortion of the word "Puritanism"; many of his contemporaries would have accepted Mencken's definition of Puritanism as constituting the core of the national tradition. Mencken himself agreed that it was the central factor in the American tradition, but, in his final myth inversion, he condemned it as dangerous and stultifying. Puritanism, in Mencken's hands, had become a tradition that had to be destroyed.

Although almost all of Mencken's "American" articles constituted a sustained denunciation of the American character and society, one exception was "The American: His Language," the only article that dealt with an aspect of American culture that Mencken could wholeheartedly admire and praise. He believed that American speech had developed so many new words and phrases, had become so altered in syntax and pronunciation, that it was becoming a separate language. In this article of August 1913, the seed of what was to become the enduring work of his lifetime, *The American Language*, Mencken dropped the satirical tone that dominated the rest of the series in the *Smart Set*. "The distinguished trait of the American is simply his tendency to use slang without any false sense of impropriety, his eager hospitality to its most audacious novelties, his ingenuous yearning to augment the conciseness, the sprightliness, and, in particular, what may be called the dramatic punch of his language. It is ever his effort to translate ideas into terms of overt acts, to give the intellectual a visual and striking quality" (95). For a brief moment Mencken's American became an iconoclast, if not in his acts, then at least in his speech, which was "a language preeminent among the tongues of the earth for its eager hospitality to new words and no less for its compactness, its naked directness, and its disdain of all academic obfuscations and restraints" (95).

## IV   *The Two Nations*

Although Mencken became more bitter in his satire after World War I, his essentially critical attitude toward his country was formed during the prewar years. "The American" series dates the emergence of that satirical line of attack that was to make him both famous and infamous in the 1920s. What is important about these prewar articles, however, is not the almost unrelieved condemnation of American society —for it is not in the nature of satirists to be fair or objective—but the manner in which Mencken used his satire. By assiduously inverting America's most cherished myths, Mencken created a new countermyth, a negative image of the American as *homo boobiens*—the citizen as mob-man. This powerful but distorted myth emerged time and again in his writings in the 1920s.

This implication, that the weakness of the American lay in the very essence of Americanism, gave a tremendous impetus to Mencken's satire, but it also created a serious artistic and intellectual problem for him. All satirists dredge up the evils and follies of their societies. Some, unfortunately, choose scapegoats from among minority groups to bear the burden of those evils. Others, like Sinclair Lewis, concoct national sterotypes—such as Babbitt, the business man, or Elmer Gantry, the evangelist—to personify folly. Some, like Mencken, create a negative image of their country, an anticountry that is distilled from all the society's shortcomings and offenses. Few satirists, however, have gone as far as Mencken in identifying by name this antination as their own country. The lands in which Gulliver traveled resembled with painful clarity Jonathan Swift's Great Britain, but Swift never actually labeled those lands "England" and "Ireland." He maintained the necessary artistic distance between reality and his satiric vision.

Mencken, then, took the ultimate step as a social satirist. He herded the fools and follies of his country into a cage and labeled the cage "America." But if America was in the cage, where was the satirist standing as he viewed the show? If everything that Mencken disliked in his society was American, then by what means could he identify and defend those national virtues that he did admire and to which he was deeply commited? Mencken was in danger of being isolated by his own rhetorical gesture—a gesture that was indeed rhetorical. The "American" articles were not the result of a deep sense of alienation from America; they were the product of Mencken's impetuous impatience, his elitist arrogance, and his satiric instinct for the jugular. Therefore, he inverted the American's myths about himself, but not his ideals. Mencken denied that Americans were freedom-loving, intelligent, honorable, or courageous; but he did not condemn the values of freedom, intelligence, honor, or courage. Moreover, when he dealt with the American language, he momentarily changed from critic to celebrant of *another* America—of one different from the one that emerged from his other articles. It was not merely language that Mencken was praising: he was covertly expressing his admiration for some of those American traits—audaciousness, conciseness, liveliness, impatience with formalism and restraint—that his newly adopted satiric persona did not allow him to recognize as belonging to American society as a whole.

Mencken's problem, then, was that he had unconsciously impoverished his vocabulary. He had made the word "American" stand for everything he was against; and, as a result, he later found it difficult to revalue the word when he wished to defend those national values to which he was deeply attached. He had, in effect, created two nations: the America of his satiric image that he overtly attacked, and an America that he covertly loved and wanted to preserve. Unfortunately, World War I was to magnify the weaknesses of the first and to make him even more unconscious of his involvement in the second.

## V  *The War*

Mencken, writing in the "Free Lance" on August 4, 1914, greeted the outbreak of World War I with this pronouncement: "War is a good thing because it is honest, because it admits the central fact of human nature. Its great merit is that it affords a natural, normal and undisguised outlet for that complex of passions and energies which civilization seeks so fatuously to hold in check. . . ." This remark seems shocking today. One must recall, however, that many educated and sincere people, on both sides of the Atlantic, held this tragically fallacious belief in the power of war to purge society of the complexities that seemed to engulf it. Idealists of the Genteel Tradition, confident that America would not become involved in the fighting, could afford to greet the war with a kind of wistful longing. In fact, President John Grier Hibbon of Princeton University feared that neutral America might be denied the spiritual and cultural chastening that Europe was about to experience. Novelist Robert Herrick was sure that the young men who were dying in Flanders had "drunk deeper than we can dream of life."[12] Mencken, of course, did not see the problem in such spiritually shimmering terms; for he wrote in the "Free Lance" of August 4, 1914, that "The American people, too secure in their isolation and grown too fat in their security, show all the signs of deteriorating national health. . . ." While Europeans were "preparing to fight out the great fight that must inevitably select and determine, in man no less than among protozoa, the fittest to survive," Americans were surrendering their ruthless vigor and their joy of life for a false idealism and repressive moralism.

This tendency of American intellectuals to use the war as a means of focusing attention on the social and cultural tensions within their own society suggests why the war years, even before America's direct involvement in the fighting, were a time of cultural crisis for the country. The ethnic diversity of the society was enough to insure that Americans would be divided in their sympathies for the belligerents. Among the intellectuals, however, powerful cultural loyalties, rather than ethnic ties, governed their sympathies toward one side or the other. Many Americans, like many Europeans, were convinced that the war was a struggle in which the very survival of civilization was at stake. Thus, depending on whether they believed in the ideals of Anglo-American "culture" or of Germanic *Kultur,* they identified with either the Allies or the Central Powers. The dominant voice in this cultural debate in America was that of the Genteel Tradition, which was naturally sympathetic to Britain, the cultural motherland. Moreover, under increasing pressure from the young rebels in art and literature, the defenders of the old Genteel order found it all too easy to see Germany as the source for all of the literary and philosophical heresies they were so earnestly combating in America.

Mencken, of course, identified with German culture those artistic and iconoclastic values that he had been championing for almost a decade. In doing so, he was not merely responding to his own ethnic heritage. He had never taken an interest in German-American organizations, and most of his previous comments on Imperial Germany had been objective and disinterested. The kaiser and the reich did not stir him, but he did respond to that Nietzschean, Romantic view of *Kultur* that had been reenforced upon his imagination by his visit to Germany in 1912. "There can be no doubt," he wrote to Elery Sedgwick," that Neitzscheism has been superimposed upon the old, unintelligent Prussian absolutism . . . ."[13]

In an article entitled "The Mailed Fist and its Prophet," published in Sedgwick's *Atlantic Monthly* in November 1914, Mencken insisted that Nietzsche's *Herrenmoral* was "hailed by all the exponets of new order as the voice of the true German Spirit . . . a perfect statement of theory and practice of sound progress" (601). This new order was no longer the old aristocracy of the court and the barracks but a new aristocracy, an "Athenian democracy" of "the laboratory, the study and the shop." A "democracy at the top" with experts instead of vote-hungry politicians in command, this New Germany was "the great test of the gospel of strength, of great daring, of efficiency" (607).

Conversely, Mencken saw England as the champion of ill-directed democracy, sentimentality, and moralism. Writing in the "Free Lance" of September 29, 1914, he stated: "For the manly, stand-up, ruthless, truth-telling, clean-minded England of another day I have the highest respect and reverence. It was an England of sound ideals and men. But for the smug, moralizing, disingenuous England of Churchill and Lloyd-George, . . . England, by Gladstone out of Pecksniff, I have no respect whatever. Its victory over Germany in this war would be a victory for all the ideas and ideals that I most ardently detest, and upon which, in my remote mud-puddle, I wage a battle with all the strength I can muster . . . ."

The battle became much more fierce than Mencken could have anticipated. Outraged by the successful Allied propaganda that depicted the Germans as barbarous Huns, Mencken undertook to portray the German side of the war. Although he continued to print attacks against himself in the column next to the "Free Lance," he soon discovered that a free and open discussion of the war was going to be difficult, if not impossible. Pro-Allied sympathy, played upon by Britain's increasingly effective propaganda machine, was produc-

ing strong anti-German sentiment, even in Baltimore. The un-
abashed *"hoch, hoch, dreimal hoch!"* with which the "Free Lance"
greeted news of each German victory was more than most of the
readers of the *Sun* could bear. Nor did many of them appreciate
Mencken's contention that President Wilson's declaration of American neutrality was essentially dishonest because it allowed Britain's
control of the seas to channel American material exclusively into the
Allied camp. The *Sun*'s management, Wilsonian and pro-Allied itself, was under great pressure to control Mencken. Finally, in late
October of 1915, the "Free Lance" was killed. The debate over the
war had turned into a question of free speech, and Mencken had
lost.

Respecting the position of his employers, Mencken contributed
occasional non-political pieces to the *Sun*. Then, in December 1916,
the paper sent him to Germany to cover the war on the eastern
front. His tour was cut short, however, by the break in diplomatic
relations between Germany and the United States. He left Germany in January 1917, stopping off in Cuba to cover a sudden and
brief revolution there. Back in Baltimore, he discovered that most of
his dispatches from Germany had been suppressed. With a declaration of war against the Central Powers imminent, he and the *Sun*
parted company.

Efforts to write for other journals became increasingly difficult.
He tried to contribute some satirical pieces to the *Atlantic Monthly*
but found it impossible. "It is, in fact, out of the question for a man
of my training and sympathies to avoid the war," he told Sedgwick,
the editor. "How can I preach upon the dangerous hysterias of
democracy without citing the super-obvious spy scare, with its typical putting of public credulity to political and personal uses. . . ."[14]
For a while, Mencken did manage to write a series of literary pieces
for the New York *Evening Mail;* but when that paper folded as the
result of a charge of espionage against its management, Mencken's
only outlet remained the nonpolitical *Smart Set*.

Mencken's support of Germany prior to 1917 was a direct outgrowth of the cultural values he had been propagating well before
the war. He had never intended to champion Germany's interests
above those of his own country, and he denied that he held any
political loyalty to Germany. "The fact is that my 'loyalty' to Germany, as a state or nation, is absolutely nil," he wrote in reply to a
correspondent in 1918. "It would do me no good whatsoever if the

Germans conquered all of Europe; it would do me a lot of damage if they beat the United States. But I believe I was right when I argued that unfairness to them was discreditable and dangerous to this country, and I am glad I did it."[15]

The experience of being silenced and spied upon during the war so embittered Mencken, that his note of alienation from American society, largely a rhetorical one in 1913, now took on a new depth. He resented the suppression of free speech and the attacks on German-Americans. Before the "Free Lance" was closed down, he warned, on February 16, 1915, that German-Americans were being pushed into "a separateness which, before the war, had never marked them." It was useless, he claimed, "to denounce them for imaginary offences against their Americanism; they have already received plain notice that they stand in a separate class, and haven't the rights of other Americans."

The war years were unfortunate in another way for Mencken. Since he lacked the capacity to submit his opinions to critical reevaluation, the war simply reenforced the negative image of America that he had created in 1913. It made him believe, moreover, that he was indeed an outsider. In his "Autobiographical Notes" written in 1925, he claimed that the experience gained from the war had benefited him. "I was being purged of the last remaining vestiges of patriotic feeling. Since then I have viewed the United States objectively, and without the slightest sentiment. . . . It was a great joy to be thus set free" (188). Mencken was wrong. Far from being set free from his concern for his country he was more involved after 1914 with America than he would ever allow himself to realize.

CHAPTER 5

# The Battle of the Books, 1914–1924

WHILE World War I affected every aspect of American life, it most severely affected the national culture. In the emotionally charged atmosphere of the war years, cultural tensions, which had been building within the society for a generation, were suddenly unleashed with such ferocity that it was not until the mid-1920s that they finally subsided. Questions of artistic traditions, esthetic values, and literary style were transformed into questions involving patriotism and even ethnicity. The literary debates, in fact, became so overheated during the decade from 1914 to 1924 that they have been refered to as the "Battle of the Books."[1] This cultural struggle was an extremely complex affair, and any attempt to impose too much clarity and order upon it risks oversimplification. Nevertheless, it can be said that at the center of the fray stood the Genteel Tradition, the dominant cultural construct of the post–Civil War era. This American version of Victorian culture had survived, seemingly intact, into the new century. Beginning around 1908, however, the challenge to the hegemony of the Genteel Tradition increased year by year until 1914, when the country was shaken by the outbreak of the World War. Intensely Anglophilic, many of the custodians of the Genteel Tradition—the established novelists, artists, poets, editors, publishers, and professors—could not resist the temptation to see in Imperial Germany the source of all of the philosophic Materialism and the literary Naturalism that seemed to threaten Genteel concepts. Nor could they resist the equally tempting tendency to brand as unpatriotic and under alien influence those writers, artists, and critics at home who seemed hostile to the Anglo-American tradition. By 1917, when America entered the war against Germany, the Genteel Tradition was prepared to see that the war to make the world safe for democracy abroad became a struggle to make culture safe for Gentility at home.

67

Those arrayed against the Genteel Tradition represented a wide spectrum of opinion and ideas and may be roughly divided into two groups: those on the cultural right who wanted a homogeneous national culture based on discipline and conservative ideals; and those on the left who wanted a pluralistic culture that would encourage diversity and would liberate, rather than discipline, the human spirit. The group on the right that stands out most clearly was the New Humanists, the principal spokesmen off which were Paul Elmer More, Irving Babbitt, and, during the war years, Stuart Pratt Sherman. These critics rejected the Genteel Tradition because they felt it had compromised the cause of cultural conservatism through its over-optimistic confidence in progress, its shallow sentimentality, and its Romantic idealism. This small, but highly articulate group of Humanists was, naturally, equally antagonistic toward the cultural rebels on the left.

While the New Humanists were a fairly cohesive group with clearly expressed ideas, the rebels on the left were much less unified. In politics, their ideas ran from the vaguely liberal to the vaguely radical. Intellectually, their work included the sharp, probing criticisms of Randolph Bourne and the nebulous, Whitman-esque effusions of Vachel Lindsay. Within their ranks were such diverse talents as those of Floyd Dell, Margaret Anderson, Van Wyck Brooks, Marianne Moore, Sherwood Anderson, Max Eastman, Carl Sandburg, and Walter Lippmann. Nevertheless, according to Henry F. May in *The End of American Innocence*, these men and women, mostly of the younger generation, held enough opinions and goals in common to constitute what May denotes as "the Rebellion." Their rebellion was, as May suggests, an "innocent" or a "cheerful" one. It was innocent in the sense that the rebels retained a highly optimistic and idealistic view of life. In fact, May goes so far as to suggest that the rebellion unconsciously accepted the cultural framework of the Genteel Tradition, but it redefined such concepts as progress, morality, idealism, and the arts in new and radical ways.[2] As Walter Lippmann put it in 1914, *"The rebel program is stated.* Scientific invention and blind social currents have made the old authority impossible in fact, the artillery fire of the iconoclasts has shattered its prestige. We inherit a rebel tradition."[3]

Mencken was not a member of the rebellion. While his relationship with the rebellion will be discussed in more detail in Chapter 6, at this point it is only necessary to note that his suspicion of democracy and his relatively pessimistic view of life kept him immune from the philosophical innocence of the younger generation. He was his own voice in the cultural struggle of the war years, but that voice was raised consistently against both the Genteel Tradition and the New Humanists. It sounded such enthusiastic support for the younger rebels that, for a time, the fact that he fought under his own flag went unnoticed by most of his contemporaries, friend and foe alike.

The almost phenomenal critical reputation that Mencken was to enjoy during the 1920s was primarily due to his prominent involvement in the "Battle of the Books." His book on Nietzsche and his reviews in the *Smart Set* had made him an important figure in the cultural skirmishing that occurred prior to 1914. When he and George Jean Nathan assumed the editorship of the magazine in that year, Mencken was in a position to add literary patronage to the influence of his reviews. In order to understand Mencken's role in the "Battle of the Books," it is necessary to consider the principal issues as he saw them: Puritanism, Humanism, the ethnic question, the role of the artist in America, the validity of the Anglo-American tradition, and the question of a usable past.

### I   *Puritanism*

Although the *Smart Set* provided Mencken with a platform for his literary, if not his political, ideas, the single most important factor in establishing his reputation as a dissident critic during the war was *A Book of Prefaces* (1917). His first real book of literary criticism and probably his best, this book contained four essays. The first three dealt with figures with whom Mencken had in one way or another closely associated himself: Joseph Conrad, Theodore Dreiser, and James Gibbons Huneker. The last essay, "Puritanism As a Literary Force," was the longest and, at the time, the most important piece because it was one of the most aggressive documents that was filed on behalf of the cultural revolt and because it gave the book its overall unity. Taken as a whole, *A Book of Prefaces* was a gauntlet thrown down before all those who sought to impede the progress of American letters.

The final essay in the book is built around two themes. The first theme, the development of Puritanism as the dominant literary and cultural tradition in America, was drawn largely from one of

Mencken's earlier articles in "The American" series. The second theme was censorship, which Mencken contended was nothing less than Puritanism writ large in the nation's law books. Now that Puritanism was under attack, censorship and moral legislation were called into play to defeat the enemy at the gates. By citing specific cases and court decisions, Mencken was able to depict Puritanism as a formidible obstacle to the emergence of a modern American literature. Refering to his own experience as a magazine editor, he claimed that before he could consider the artistic merits of a story submitted to him, he had to ask himself "whether its publication will be permitted—not even whether it is intrinsically good or evil, moral or immoral, but whether some roving Methodist preacher, self-commissioned to keep watch on letters, will read indecency into it. Not a week passes that I do not decline some sound and honest piece of work for no other reason" (277). Although the tone of the essay was pessimistic, it was nonetheless a call to arms. "We have yet no delivery, but we have at least the beginnings of a revolt, or, at all events, of a protest. . . . Maybe a new day is not quite so far off as it seems to be, and with it we may get our Hardy, our Conrad, our Swinburne . . . our Moore, our Meredith and our Synge"(282–83).

With the possible exception of Van Wyck Brooks, Mencken did more than any other critic to make Puritanism a central issue in the cultural debates of the 1910s and 1920s. In doing so, Brooks and Mencken obscured more than they clarified. Because their Puritanism was not defined with genuine historical accuracy, it tended to become a bogey in the minds of the younger generation of writers.

Why then did Mencken choose this label to identify the cultural forces that he sought to overthrow? Basically, the label was chosen for him by his opponents; for both the defenders of the Genteel Tradition and the New Humanists looked vaguely to the Puritan heritage as the foundation of American culture. The New Humanists were even more insistent on seeing the Puritan spirit as essential to the survival of proper civilized values. To Paul Elmer More, in particular, Puritanism was *the* American tradition: it was the source of moral restraint and discipline that enabled the individual to preserve his inner spirit amid the alluring but dangerous demands of nature.

Mencken agreed that Puritanism was basic to the American tradition. Typically, however, he stood the argument on its head by revealing Puritanism not as a vital but as an unhealthy force. If Puritanism was centered on morality, then morality itself was repressive and destructive. If Puritanism had produced the best in American culture, then American culture was a stunted and twisted growth. If Puritanism was *the* American tradition, then the national tradition smelled of sickness and decay. Puritanism, in Mencken's hands, became an *un*usable past.

Mencken was thus drawn, perhaps unwittingly, into an attack on the American past. The proponents of the Genteel Tradition and of the New Humanism, having staked out the past in their own terms, made it seem a burden to Mencken and the literary rebels like Van Wyck Brooks and Randolph Bourne. Instead of questioning the conservative reading of the past, Mencken and the other opponents of Puritanism slipped into a pattern frequently seen in American cultural history: the proponents of a new culture accepted the terms of the debate as presented to them by the old guard. As a result, the cultural rebellion fell all too easily into seeing itself as simply the anti-Puritan reversal of the Puritan image.

This problem was exacerbated by another factor, also typical of American cultural rebels: a surprising ignorance of the past. Even Van Wyck Brooks, one of the few rebels who recognized immediately the need to build the new literature on the foundation of a tradition, tended to work against his own goal because he lacked a deep, sound understanding of the American literary past.[4] As a result, his books were so damning in their portrayal of that past that he was unconvincing in his suggestions as to how (or even why) the bridge of tradition could be rebuilt. Mencken was in an even more difficult position, since his awareness of American literary history was more superficial than Brooks'. Moreover, he was so preoccupied with the Puritan ogre that not until the 1920s was he convinced of the need to tie the rebellion to a national tradition. Even then, he lacked both the knowledge and the sustaining interest in the problem to do more than sketch a possible connection between past and present.

## II  *Humanism*

The "Battle of the Books" was so confused and impassioned that American critics often seemed to maneuver in those dim areas where "ignorant armies clash by night." A most striking example is found in Mencken's protracted debate with the New Humanists.

Although it was but a preliminary to what became known as the "Humanist Controversy" during the late 1920s and early 1930s, it was, unfortunately, one of Mencken's major concerns—unfortunate, because Mencken misunderstood or choose to misrepresent much of the Humanist position and thereby added to an atmosphere already marred by ignorance on all sides.[5]

Mencken carelessly assumed that the intense conservatism of Babbitt, More, and, for a time, Sherman made them the most articulate spokesmen for the Genteel Tradition. He was quite wrong. The fact that the Humanists attacked the Genteel Tradition as vehemently from the right as did the younger writers from the left never seems to have dawned upon the Baltimore critic. Nor did he recognize how many attitudes he shared with the Humanists. Elitist, suspicious of democracy, and economically conservative, Mencken and the Humanists were also similar in their dislike of sentimentality, optimism, shallow idealism, and moralism.

There were, however, several issues that did create a deep and genuine gulf between them. The Humanists, rooted in their Classical training, rejected the idea of cultural liberation for both the arts and the human spirit. To them, civilization was possible only through the imposition of a rigid control on the natural instincts by continual introspective restraint. When Babbitt preached his idea of the "inner check" and More his *frein vital,* both hoped to keep the dangerous human ego on a short tether. To them, this restraining influence could take hold only in a culture committed to tradition. For Babbitt this was the tradition of Classicism; for More and Sherman, it was the tradition of Puritanism.

Following the point of view he had expressed in his books about Shaw and about Nietzsche, Mencken believed in the free, untrammeled play of the ego. Moreover, just as his political conservatism was tempered by a libertarianism that the Humanists would have found dangerous, so his attitude toward culture was quite radical in comparison to theirs. To Mencken, culture was not to be bound to tradition but was to be allowed to evolve freely. Because such an evolving culture had to reflect contemporary needs and attitudes, Mencken naturally rejected the Humanist attempt to impose preconceived and rigid standards upon the arts and on literature. "To More and Babbitt," he wrote in *Prejudices: Second Series,* "only death can atone for the primary offense of the artist" (22).

### III    *The Ethnic Issue*

Despite Mencken's efforts to tempt the two scholars into a direct public debate with him during this period, More and Babbitt refused to be drawn. It remained to Sherman, Babbitt's pupil and More's protégé, to cross swords with the Baltimore iconoclast. The result not only continued the generation of more heat than light but also helped focus the literary war on the volatile topic of ethnicity. Mencken himself must share some of the blame for this development, in spite of the fact that he had been a victim of the ethnic issue during the war. His tendency to identify as "foreign" those qualities of excellence he found in American writing helped to highlight the non-Anglo-Saxon background of such writers as Dreiser and Huncker. Mencken's own celebrations of Central European culture made it all too easy for overzealous patriots to focus on his German-American origins and to question his allegiance.

Although Stewart Pratt Sherman was by no means the most virulent of those who used the ethnic attack, his ability to command space in such prestigious journals as the *Nation* and his power as a polemicist (which at times rivaled Mencken's) made him a dangerous foe during the war. The ex-professor of English who had turned critic did not enter the "Battle of the Books" against Mencken directly. His initial target was Mencken's friend, Theodore Driser, who was also a German-American. Sherman condemned Dreiser's Naturalism as alien to the moral vision of the American Puritan heritage.[6] Unfortunately, in a review of Dreiser's *The Genius* in the December 2, 1915, issue of the *Nation*, Sherman sarcastically pilloried the novelist's work as representative of "a new note in American literature, coming from that 'ethnic' element of our mixed population which . . . is to redeem us from Puritanism and insure our artistic salvation" (648).

Mencken, who was soon actively engaged in helping to organize a writers' protest against the subequent banning of *The Genius*, eventually replied on Dreiser's behalf in 1917, first in an article in *Seven Arts* and then in *Prefaces*. Typically, he turned from a defense of Dreiser to an attack on Sherman. "I single out Dr. Sherman," he wrote in *Prefaces*, "not because his pompous syllogisms have any plausibility in fact or logic, but simply because he may well stand as archetype of the booming, indignant corrupter of criteria, the moralist turned critic. . . . What offends him is not actually Dreiser's shortcomings as an artist, but Dreiser's shortcomings as a Christian and an American" (138).

When Sherman reviewed Mencken's *Prefaces* in the *Nation* in November 29, 1917, he stressed the ethnic theme by depicting Mencken and those associated with him as a part of a Hunnish plot against American culture. To link together men with names like Huneker, Ludwig Lewisohn, Louis Untermeyer, Peter Viereck, Dreiser, George Jean Nathan, and Alfred Knopf (Mencken's publisher) was hardly of innocent intent in the heady days of 1917. To Sherman, Mencken's "continuous laudation of a Teutonic-Oriental pessimism and nihilism in philosophy . . . of the *Herrenmoral*, and of anything but Anglo-Saxon civilization, is not precisely and strictly *aesthetic* criticism; an unsympathetic person might call it infatuated propagandism" (594). Mencken considered such attacks on himself and Dreiser as "hitting below the belt," for he found it was almost impossible to reply to them in an atmosphere dominated by patriotic hysteria and censorship. He maintained a grim silence and waited for the war to end.[7]

The Mencken-Sherman debate was renewed vigorously in 1919 when the latter reviewed Mencken's *Prejudices: First Series*. Sherman satirically depicted Mencken as the barbarous spokesman of the cultureless descendents of the immigrant masses—the "Loyal Independent Order of United Hiberno-German-Anti-English Americans."[8] Although the war was over, the rising demand for an end to immigration put a nasty edge on Sherman's sentiments. Now, however, Mencken decided to meet the ethnic issue head on. In *Prejudices: Second Series*, published the following year, he avidly admitted that the American cultural tradition, as defined by Sherman, was indeed under attack from the non-Anglo-Saxon part of the population. Standing Sherman's Anglo-Saxonism on its head, he predicted that the so-called ethnic writers would eventually triumph because the Anglo-Saxon was culturally inferior. Without "this rebellion of immigrant iconoclasts," Mencken concluded, "the whole body of national literature would tend to sink to the 100% [American] level . . ."(50).

This introduction of ethnicity into literary criticism was not quite so irresponsible or even so unedifying as it might seem. Because critics of the time did not divorce art from society, their criticism reflected the very real cultural debates of their society. One question, which seems endemic in American history, revolved around the very nature of culture: should it be homogeneous in its character or reflect a pluralism of values and ideas? Sherman, who was among those who believed in cultural homogeneity, sincerely felt that it was necessary and desirable that all Americans conform to the values of the Puritan tradition. Mencken, who spoke for cultural pluralism, demanded the right to diversity: all groups and all individuals in America should be free from the pressure of conformity. "Laws are passed to hobble and cage the citizen of the newer stocks in a hundred fantastic ways," he wrote in *Prejudices: Fourth Series* (1924). "Every divergence from the norm of the low-caste Anglo-Saxon is treated as an *attentat* against the commonwealth and is punished with eager ferocity" (30). Mencken was so eager to document the downfall of Anglo-Saxon culture that he urged novelist Percy Marks to make a study of the grandparents of contemporary American writers. "The inquiry would show, I believe, that there has been a steady displacement of the Anglo-Saxon strain."[9]

## IV The Lonesome Artist

The ethnic argument was not the only point at issue between Mencken and Sherman, for they also disagreed about the nature of the relationship between the artist and his society. Sherman spoke for a strong popular tradition in American literature when he called upon the artist to "express the profound moral idealism of America" and to "slip a spiritual goldpiece into the palm of each of his fellow countrymen."[10] Mencken, however, believed that the artist's role was to question, not reinforce, the dominant values of American society. The artist-iconoclast was at war with his society, which, if he was a genuine artist, was at war with him.

In a long essay entitled "The National Letters" in the second book of *Prejudices*, Mencken tried to diagnose the problems facing American literature. "A great literature is . . . chiefly the product of doubting and inquiring minds in revolt against the immovable certainties of the nation" (101). In America, however, the artist could rely upon no class and upon no institutions to protect and support him. The mob was against him. The press and universities were in the hands of the plutocracy, which was fearful in its turn of any dissent from the status quo. To Mencken's elitist mind, this isolation of the genuine artist suggested the real problem facing the development of American culture: "the lack of a civilized aristocracy, secure in its position, animated by an intelligent curiosity, skeptical of all facile generalizations, superior to sentimentality of the mob, and delighting in the battle of ideas for its own sake" (65). Without a real aristocracy there could be no "mantle of protection around eccentricity." The artist had to carry out his rebellion alone. He was the "lonesome artist" rejected by his society and without any allies.

Although Mencken's elitism is discussed in a later chapter, it should be noted here that this elitism represented another area of disagreement between himself and Sherman. In spite of Sherman's Humanist background, his instincts were basically those of a liberal and a democrat. Once he had escaped the passions generated by the war, Sherman's liberalism began to assert itself over the doctrines of Babbitt and More. He took a much more tolerant view of the new literature and by the time of his death in 1926, had even begun to praise some of the very authors whom Mencken himself had long supported.

## V   *Cutting the Painter*

Looking back over the "Battle of the Books" from the vantage point of 1923, Mencken believed that it had been the war that had broken the back of the Genteel Tradition. "The bald fact that the majority of the adherents of that old tradition were violent Anglomaniacs, and extravagant in their support of the English cause . . . was sufficient in itself to make most of the younger writers incline the other way. The struggle thus became a battle royal between fidelity to the English cultural heritage of the country and advocacy of a new national culture that should mirror, not only the influence of England, but also that of every country that had contributed elements to the American strain."[11]

While this statement is an oversimplification of a very complex problem, it does explain why critics in the 1910s and early 1920s were still debating the question of America's cultural independence. It also explains why Mencken, who had once been an enthusiastic champion of such English writers as Thomas Hardy and H. G. Wells, should have become almost Anglophobic in this period. In "The National Letters," he claimed that "The essence of a self-reliant and autonomous culture is an unshakable egoism. It must not only regard itself as a peer of any other culture; it must regard itself as the superior of any other" (93). American culture, however, had always existed in the shadow of England: "Here the decadent Anglo-Saxon majority still looks obediently and a bit wistfully toward the motherland. No good American ever seriously questions English judgment on an aesthetic question . . ." This situation added to the difficulties of the American artist: "Looking within himself, he finds that he is different, that he diverges from the English standard, that he is authentically American—and to be authentically American is to be officially inferior. He thus faces dismay at the very start . . ." (94). America, Mencken maintained, was a cultural colony of England; therefore, the artist was as yet undelivered by a declaration of independence in art and literature.

As usual, Mencken was exaggerating; but his anti-English tactic was useful to his critical strategy. If the defenders of the old order were going to wrap themselves in the Anglo-American tradition, Mencken was willing to turn the tables on them by portraying them as antinationalistic colonials. At the same time Mencken's own sense of cultural nationalism was very real. When it became clear that American literature was finding its own distinct voice, he jubilantly proclaimed that British writers had fallen behind their American cousins. When British novelist Hugh Walpole took issue with this view in an open letter in the *Bookman* in 1925, Mencken merely intoned, "If I violate English pruderies I can only regret it politely. I am not an English-man but an American." "The Republic," he announced, "has cut the painter, and has begun to go it alone."[12]

Fortunately, Mencken's most powerful and original contribution to the controversy over the Anglo-American literary tradition went far beyond the limits of polemics. In 1919, he published the first edition of what was eventually to become his most enduring work, *The American Language.* Expanding an idea originally expressed in "The American" articles, Mencken intended the work to be another salvo in the "Battle of the Books."[13] The very title challenged the old assumptions of the strong cultural ties between Britain and America. American speech, Mencken predicted, was developing its own vocabulary and syntax to such an extent that it would eventually be a separate langauge and one totally incomprehensible to an Englishman. Here was cultural nationalism with a vengeance.

By describing how American speech had taken on a life of its own despite ridicule· from abroad and pedagogical strictures at home, Mencken was also putting forward a concept of language that was hotly disputed by conservative scholars. In line with his literary criticism, Mencken saw language as a continually evolving phenomenon that constantly reflected social change and the contemporary face of culture. The attempt to fix it to unchanging laws of grammar and other academic restraints not only was futile but denied the richness and inventiveness—the very Americanness—of the language.

Naturally, Mencken was an unrepentant and enthusiastic defender of slang. "Given the poet," he wrote hopefully in the first edition of *The American Language,* "there may suddenly come a day when our *theirins* and *would'a hads* will take on the barbaric stateliness of the peasant locutions of old Maurya in Synge's 'Riders to the Sea.' " It was wrong, Mencken maintained, to view slang as grotesque or the people who used it as absurd. "In all human beings, if only understanding be brought to the business, dignity will be found, and that dignity cannot fail to reveal itself, soon or late, in the words and phrases with which they make known their high hopes and aspirations and cry out against the intolerable meaninglessness of life" (321).

Neither Mencken nor his publisher, Knopf, expected *The American Language* to sell many copies. Nevertheless, coming as it did at the end of World War I and at a time when the "Battle of the Books" was beginning to attract the awareness of the popular audience, the first printing was rapidly sold. As hundreds of contributors from all over the country sent him material about local usages, Mencken began to expand the work. A revised edition appeared in 1921 and a third revised edition in 1923. Mencken again rewrote and enlarged the book in 1936 and followed it with two supplements in the 1940s. [14]

In the "Preface" to the 1936 edition, Mencken had to admit that his prediction of the parting of the ways of American and British English had not occurred. But he remained adamant in his cultural nationalism. The connection between the two modes of speech had remained unbroken because British English was becoming "a kind of dialect of American, just as the language spoken by the American was once a dialect of English" (vi).

*The American Language* is a work of solid, painstaking research and a compilation of voluminous primary materials contributed by correspondents, among whom were many eminent academicians. Although some philologists and linguists have viewed Mencken's work as, at best, that of a gifted amateur, Mencken's intention had not been to put himself forward as a specialist. The value of his work lies in its attempt at synthesis. Yet his success produced something more than a gloss on the work of professional language scholars. As a historian of language, Mencken was also a historian of an important aspect of American culture. That he produced such a brilliant and original work years before American cultural history had become a recognized and established field is merely one token of his achievement.

## VI   *The Iconoclastic Tradition*

D. C. Stenerson has pointed out that *"The American Language* reinforced Mencken's efforts to create an American as opposed to an Anglo-Saxon tradition."[15] Certainly, by the end of the war Mencken seems to have been aware of the need to establish the concept of an American literary tradition that could act as an alternative to those supported by the Genteel Tradition and the Humanists. By allowing his opponents to set the terms of the debate, Mencken had come close to rejecting the very idea of a national tradition in letters. This stand had led him into the contradictory position of calling for a national literature while at the same time defining all of the superior qualities in the new writing as alien.

Although Mencken took a while to put together his own version of the American tradition, its shape is suggested in the essay on "The National Letters." Looking about the literary scene, Mencken saw "an undercurrent of revolt" against the "intrinsic childishness of the Puritan *Anschauung.* The remedy for that childishness is skepticism, and already skepticism shows itself: in the iconoclastic political realism of Harold Stearns, Waldo Frank and company, in the groping questions of Dreiser, Cabell, Anderson . . ." (100). Mencken's task was to project this tendency toward cultural and literary revolt back into the past. He did this in a negative way in the essay when he depicted Poe, Whitman, Hawthorne, and other nineteenth century writers as "lonesome artists" who had been ignored or misunderstood in their own country and who had thereby been forced to work and think in isolation. Even earlier, in *Prejudices: First Series* in an essay on Emerson, he had claimed that, despite all the enthusiasm for the Concord sage among the conservatives, America had forgotten Emerson's "unheeded law":"defer never to the popular cry" (192).

Not until Mencken wrote his final essay for the *Smart Set* in

December 1923, however, did he sketch the bare foundations of an American iconoclastic tradition. Returning again to Emerson, he could now confidently claim that "It was obviously Emerson's central aim in life to liberate the American mind—to set it free from the crippling ethical obsessions of Puritanism, to break down herd thinking, to make liberty more real on the intellectual plane that it could ever be on the political plane." Although Emerson had become a sort of saint in the heaven of Gentility, he nevertheless "paved the way for every intellectual revolt that has occurred since his time. . ." (144).

In *Prejudices: Fourth Series*, Mencken maintained that subservience to the Anglo-Saxon norm was contrary to the reality of the American cultural heritage. "The ancient American tradition . . . was obviously a tradition of individualism and revolt, not of herd-morality and conformity. If one argues otherwise, one must inevitably argue that the great men of the Golden Age were not Emerson, Hawthorne, Poe and Whitman, but Cooper, Irving, Longfellow and Whittier" (19). One may appreciate Sherman's surprise and bemusement when he noted that his opponent was now loudly calling up an American literary tradition that included some of the most respected figures in American letters. Yet all Mencken had done was to extend his tradition of iconoclasm, which he had previously found only in European literature, westward across the Atlantic. What is surprising is that it took him so long to do so. Obsessed as he was with Puritanism, it was not until the concept of the Puritan tradition was beginning to crumble that he could see the possibility and the need for an alternative reading of the past.

That Mencken responded to that need is a sign both of his cultural nationalism and of what Sherman, satirically but perceptively, denoted as his "passion" for "moral progaganda."[16] Mencken's ministry was to the young writers. As noted in the discussion of his concept of irony and pity, by the early 1920s Mencken seemed afraid that the younger writers, in their new-found freedom and in their rejection of idealism, might swing the pendulum too far in the other direction. They might be so caught up in cynicism and skepticism as to forget the essential sense of humanity upon which good literature depended. Similarly, Mencken seems to have sensed the need to focus their attention on their own country and to remind them that as rebels they were a part of a great national tradition.

Unfortunately, Mencken developed this idea too late. The "Battle of the Books" was coming to an end and with it Mencken's own interest in literature. The essay "The American Tradition" was nothing more than the sketch of an idea. Had he pursued fully the implication in the essay, he might have realized just how much he himself belonged to the tradition of the American rebel.

### CHAPTER 6

# *From the* Smart Set *to* The American Mercury, *1914—1924*

## I *The* Smart Set

THE war years would have been a much bleaker period for Mencken had it not been for the *Smart Set.* The magazine not only offered him an outlet for his writing but also enabled him to play a direct role in furthering the development of American literature. Under the co-editorship of Mencken and his partner, George Jean Nathan, the *Smart Set* became one of the best known organs of the literary rebellion.[1] The Mencken-Nathan editorship was, however, actually the second act of the *Smart Set's* involvement in the cultural foment of the period. The first act began in 1913, when Mencken talked the magazine's new owner, George Adams Thayer, into taking on Willard Huntington Wright as editor. Wright, a young West Coast critic, was already a staff member of both the *Smart Set* and *Town Topics;* he and Mencken had been attracted to each other by a mutual interest in Nietzsche and by a common hatred of Puritanism. Wright, Mencken, and Nathan, the magazine's theater critic, agreed to work in close cooperation. Although the arrangement was a sort of triumvirate, Wright undoubtedly gave the magazine his own stamp and was ultimately responsible for both its brilliant success and for the crisis that ended his brief tenure as editor.[2]

The new regime began with high hopes and a good budget. The basic idea was to try to enliven the *Smart Set* and to look at the same time for a sponsor for a new "knock-'em-down anti-Puritan" weekly. For a while everything went well. Under Wright, the *Smart Set* began to blossom with contributions from such figures as Theodore Dreiser, Louis Untermeyer, Ludwig Lewisohn, Harriet Monroe,

Robinson Jeffers, and Flloyd Dell. From Europe, material arrived from Ezra Pound, W. B. Yeats, Franz Wedekind, Arthur Schnitzler, August Strindberg, D. H. Lawrence, George Moore, and Joseph Conrad. At the same time, Mencken and Nathan sharpened their reviews and began a series of satirical articles under the joint pseudonymn of Owen Hatteras. The whole magazine gained a reputation for excellence, innovation, and satiric bravura.

Unfortunately, Wright's initial success and enthusiasm led him to ignore the sensibilities of his readers and of his publisher, Thayer, who was soon appalled by the rising costs and by the falling circualtion. Although the "sex" stories Wright printed seem tame by present-day standards, they were daring enough in 1913. In fact, Mencken was soon counseling more discretion and less sensation. The war against the Puritan could not be turned into a war against the readers. By the end of the year, Thayer had become impossible to placate; Wright refused to comprise, and Mencken suggested that editor and owner part company.

Wright left the magazine in January 1914; and, for a brief period, the *Smart Set*, under the editorship of Mark Lee Luther, became, in Mencken's words, "as righteous and decrepit as a converted madame." Thayer soon sold the magazine, and the new management offered the editor's chair to Nathan. When Nathan insisted that Mencken be made co-editor, this idea was accepted; and the *Smart Set* entered its most famous decade in the summer of 1914. Since Mencken still refused to leave Baltimore, Nathan, who refused to live anywhere but New York, became the senior editor who supervised most of the routine editing. Mencken, who was primarily responsible for soliciting material and who was first reader, selected the manuscripts to send to his partner. Each editor had a veto over what went into the magazine. Mencken made regular trips to New York to help work out the final details for each issue.

Even without the difficulties that World War I was soon to impose in terms of rising paper costs and the threat of censorship, the vehicle that Mencken and Nathan inherited was far from promising. Unlike the little magazines, such as the *Little Review*, the *Dial*, *Poetry*, and the *Masses*, whose reliance upon philanthropic backers made them independent of popular tastes, the *Smart Set* was and remained a commercial venture. As such it was unique among the periodicals of the rebellion. Not only was the magazine supposed to make a profit, but, since Mencken and Nathan accepted stock in lieu of part of their salary, their own livelihood was invested in the magazine's survival.

This factor placed the editors in a difficult position. The funds at their disposal were very limited. At the same time, Wright's debacle clearly illustrated that the *Smart Set* was tied to a readership with only a limited toleration for the wilder shores of anti-Puritanism. To turn the *Smart Set* into the kind of magazine the editors wanted meant attracting a new audience, but their doing so also meant holding the magazine's old readers long enough to survive the transition. The problem was never really solved; subscriptions continued to decline; and the *Smart Set* remained, for Mencken in particular, a halfway house, a curious mixture of iconoclasm and sophisticated conventionality. The compromise that Mencken and Nathan hit upon was a combination of snobbery, satire, and real solid literary achievement. In an attempt to hold on to its traditional readership, the editors sought to cultivate an elitist image for the magazine. "A Polite Magazine for Polite People"; "A Magazine of Cleverness"; "We don't buy names, we make them"—these were some of the mottos that appeared on the *Smart Set*'s covers and in advertisements in hopes of capturing the snobbish sophisticate.

Like elitism, satire was an extension of the personality and styles of the editors themselves. Not only did satire constitute one-fifth of the *Smart Set*'s contents, it was the main ingredient in the style of both Mencken's and Nathan's performance as editors. They ran the magazine with a showmanlike combination of cabaret and burlesque that could not have failed to attract attention. They set up a "free lunch" table for starving poets in their garishly decorated editorial offices. Would-be contributors who pressed their cases too hard and too often were informed that either Mr. Mencken or Mr. Nathan had entered a Trappist monastery and was not available for consultation. In 1923 the editors announced their joint candidacy for the presidency (they would flip a coin to see who actually occupied the White House). Even in the darkest days, when financial restrictions forced them to marshal a stage army of noms de plume and write half the magazine themselves, satire kept the *Smart Set* afloat. As Mencken told Theodore Dreiser in 1915, "We guess that satire would save it [the *Smart Set*] and we guessed right."[3]

Meanwhile, both editors were anxious to fill the magazine with as much good writing as their meager budget could attract. Through their policy of making prompt decisions about manuscripts and of immediate payment, they did manage to attract considerable talent from two sources. Because of their much publicized war against gentility and conventionality, the editors could get that sort of material from established writers, American and foreign, which would not fit into more popular and respectable periodicals. In addition, the *Smart Set* did have one advantage over the avant-garde little magazines: although its rates were among the lowest in New York, it did pay something, whereas the little magazines were largely mutual charity efforts on behalf of editors and contributors. As a result, the *Smart Set* editors managed to publish some excerpts from James Joyce's *Dubliners* (marking his first appearance in America), Somerset Maugham's "Rain" (the original of the Sadie Thompson story), and an excerpt from James Branch Cabell's *Jurgen* (one of the most widely talked about books of the early 1920s).

Obviously such coups were hard to achieve. Therefore, a larger source of good material came from young writers for whom breaking into print (with a small check) was a driving ambition. Because the editors wisely catered to such unknowns, they made some first rate discoveries. They published three plays of Eugene O'Neill and some of F. Scott Fitzgerald's first stories, as well as articles and stories from such figures as Maxwell Anderson, Thomas Beer, S. N. Behrman, and Ben Hecht—all of whom became regular contributors. By cultivating these new writers, Mencken and Nathan made a particularly valuable contribution to the rebellion.

However, the *Smart Set*'s involvement with the rebellion had its limits, for neither editor had any time for experimental writing of any sort. The New Poetry movement passed them by completely, as did most of the avant-garde prose that followed in the wake of James Joyce's *Ulysses* (serialized by the *Little Review*). Nor did they have much sympathy for the "bread and roses" radicalism of the Marxist Bohemians. Finally, despite the editors' anti-Puritanism, both Mencken and Nathan looked askance at attempts to take the gates of prudity by a full frontal assault on sexual taboos. "No man in the world is hotter for artistic freedom than I am . . . ," Mencken once told Dreiser, "but I know that there are certain rules that can't be broken, and I am disinclined to waste time trying to break them when there is so much work to do in places where actual progress can be made."[4] Although this attitude was partly due to a concern about censorship, it was also a matter of taste, even conservatism. "My dissents," Mencken once said, "are from ideas, not from decorums. . . ."[5]

There was one area in which the *Smart Set* matched or even surpassed the efforts of the little magazines of the rebellion. Continuing a policy begun by Wright, but also reflecting Mencken's own interests, the magazine sought to introduce the new writing of Europe to Americans. Frank Harris in London, Ezra Pound in London and Paris, and Ernest Boyd in Dublin acted as scouts for overseas material. Half of this came from English and Irish writers such as Joyce, Yeats, Lord Dunsany, Padraic Colum, Maugham, Aldous Huxley, and Hugh Walpole. While few of these foreign writers were regular contributors, their work was usually of a high caliber. Carl Dolmetsch, the *Smart Set*'s historian feels that in terms of both the volume and the quality of the foreign works produced, the magazine was "unsurpassed and even unequalled" by the little magazines.[6]

## II  *Mencken and the Rebellion*

Mencken's own relationship with the rebellion is not easy to assess. As has been stressed earlier, the movement to liberate American culture was not a homogeneous one. Those involved faced a common enemy and certainly shared certain vague ideas about art and society. But, in Henry F. May's words, most of the younger rebels were "cheerful" or "innocent" in that they were generally optimistic and could superficially reconcile or even ignore deep differences within their ranks. Mencken differed on so many points from the young rebels that May dubbed him, "a somewhat older and quite separate voice in the rising chorus of the liberated."[7]

Paul Elmer More once asked Stuart Pratt Sherman, "Why do [the young liberals] and a man like Mencken consort together so readily, when as 'democrats' and 'aristocrat' they ought to be at one another's throats?"[8] Mencken's elitism obviously set him off from the majority of the rebels, who believed in the democratic spontaneity of art and whose politics were liberal or even radical. Nor did Mencken have much time for the tendency of the rebels to follow such strange gods as Henri Bergson and Sigmund Freud. Mencken's pessimistic view of the meaninglessness of life and his always present irony were not a part of the basic tone and style of the more optimistic writers of the rebellion. Their rebellious roots lay primarily in the emotional and optimistic Progressive Era in which they came of age; but

Mencken's lay in the Esthetic and Naturalistic movements of the 1890s.

Yet, for a while, a tacit accomodation existed between Mencken and the young rebels, whose cheerful innocence did not impel them to pick fights easily with those who lent them support. At the same time, Mencken's generosity to the writers and obvious commitment to the liberation of American letters overrode his suspicion of some of the flags, political and literary, under which the rebels marched. The battle against the enemy took precedence over what he would have regarded as the philosophical frivolities of writers who were so clearly in need of encouragement.

Mencken was not, however, free from criticism within the rebel ranks. A few of them, for example, felt he was too cautious about censorship. Unsympathetic with the compromises Mencken and Nathan felt obliged to make to keep the *Smart Set* afloat, Theodore Dreiser (also an older voice in the rebellion) gruffly told Mencken that "for a man with your critical point of view [,] the stuff you are publishing is not literature and there are those who are getting it under your nose," a sentiment also echoed by Ezra Pound.[9] Randolph Bourne, one of the most radical of the younger rebels, expanded on this point in his review of *Prefaces* in 1917. Noting that Mencken, by his own admission, rejected worthy stories because of his fear of the censor, Bourne asked, "But what is this but to act as busy ally to that very comstockery he denounces? If the Menckens are not going to run the risk, in the name of freedom, they are scarcely justified in trying to infect us with their own caution."[10] Bourne had a point, but so did Mencken. The *Seven Arts*, an excellent periodical with which Bourne was closely associated, folded that same year because its sponsor was frightened by the staff's refusal to temper their antiwar opinions.

In the same review, Bourne raised a question that came closer to defining the differences between Mencken and at least some of the rebels. Bourne complained, rightly, that Mencken's concentration on Puritanism was creating an ogre of exaggerated proportions. The trouble with Mencken was that he was too preoccupied with the Philistine majority, wrote Bourne. "Why cannot Demos be left alone for awhile to its commercial magazines and its mawkish novels? All good writing is produced in serene unconsciousness of what Demos desires or demands. It cannot be created at all if the artist worries about what Demos will think of him or do to him. The artist writes for that imagined audience of perfect comprehenders. The critic must judge for that audience too."[11] Writing from Europe, Ezra Pound put the same criticism to Mencken personally in a letter in 1919. Commenting on the iconoclast's *In Defense of Women* (1918), Pound scolded, "What is wrong with it, and with your work in general is that you have drifted into writing for your inferiors. . . . We have all sinned through trying to make the uneducated understand things. Certainly you will lose a great part of your public when you stop trying to civilize the waste places; and you will gain about fifteen readers."[12]

There was a good deal of truth in these criticisms. However, Bourne, Pound, and Dreiser ignored Mencken's most valuable role in the rebellion. In spite of his pose as an elitist, Mencken had no desire to turn his back on "Demos" or to seek out a small devoted coterie. His whole purpose as a critic and a writer was indeed to civilize the waste places. If this intention made him, as Bourne complained, more concerned at times with the Philistine than the artist, or, as Pound saw it, more of a popularizer and less of an intellectual, it also made Mencken a powerful figure in the "Battle of the Books." As a popularizer *and* as a critic, as the schoolmaster to the culturally unwashed *as well as* the champion of the artist, Mencken dominated for over a decade that vital middle ground of criticism where the new writing could be brought before a new and wider audience.

If, by the end of World War I, the rebels were beginning to voice doubts about Mencken, the critic was now prepared to turn his attentions to what he considered their weaknesses. In "The National Letters," he showed his disapproval of the gamier aspects of the rebellion as symbolized by the artist enclaves in Greenwich Village. He depicted the average *literatus* of the Village "in corduroy trousers and a velvet jacket, hammering furiously upon a pine table in a Macdougal street celler . . . his discourse full of insane hairsplittings about *vers libre*, futurism, spectrism, vorticism, *Expressionismus* . . ." (27). The fruits of such labors were seldom worth Mencken's notice: "I have yet to hear of a first-rate book coming out of it [the Village], or a short story of arresting quality, or even a poem of any solid distinction." The work of the young experimentalists was "jejune and imitative" (29).

Nor was Mencken pleased with the postwar tendency of the young writers to become expatriates. Although he himself was briefly tempted to leave America, his cultural nationalism soon reasserted itself.[13] In *Prejudices: Third Series* (1922), he satirically, but accurately, described his position: "Yet I remain on the dock, wrapped in the flag, when the Young Intellectuals set sail. Yet here I stand, unshaken and undespairing, a loyal and devoted Americano, even a chauvinist . . ." (11). Most of Mencken's last essays on literature were really sermons that urged the young writers to recognize the *American* rebel tradition, to focus on their own society, to draw their material from American character types.

In his last article in the *Smart Set*, in December 1923, Mencken noted that the literary battle for the liberation of letters had finally been won. But what use did the American writer make of his new opportunities? "Certainly not the worst use possible, but also certainly not the best. He is free, but he is not yet, perhaps, worthy of freedom" (142). To drive home his criticism of the young writers, he commissioned the Irish critic Ernest Boyd to write a devastating, satirical composite portrait of the "aesthetes" for the first issue of the new *American Mercury*. When Boyd's "Aesthete: Model 1924" appeared in the January 1924 issue, its contents infuriated its victims, and they bombarded the unfortunate Boyd for days with epithets and stink bombs. They even published a single issue little magazine, *Aesthete: 1925*, the following year, which was full of anti-Mencken barbs.[14] The old literary alliances of the "Battle of the Books" had come to an end.

### III   *The Literary Legacy*

The rebellion itself was a phenomenon of the 1910s. New literary alignments took place in the 1920s, and although Mencken largely abandoned literary criticism in 1924, he nevertheless left his imprint on the writing of that decade. His influence was, admittedly, limited to certain types of writers; his lack of understanding of and sympathy for those experimenting in new forms had cut him off from a number of the younger artists. But on authors like Sinclair Lewis, F. Scott Fitzgerald, and a number of lesser lights who contributed short stories to the *Mercury*, Mencken's influence was powerful and at times direct. In his biography of Sinclair Lewis, Mark Schorer perhaps exaggerates when he claims that Mencken's concept of Puritanism provided "not only Sinclair Lewis but all the writers of the twenties with a platform from which they could take their literary pot shots at American culture." Nevertheless, Schorer's statement does suggest the manner in which Mencken's literary legacy operated; for as he points out, Mencken helped Lewis focus on "the standardization of manners in a business culture and the stultification of morals in middle-class convention." In a similar vein, a Fitzgerald scholar has suggested that "Mencken deepened Fitzgerald's understanding of American society. . . ."[15]

The nature of that understanding was certainly limited. One must bear in mind, however, that the postwar period was, intellectually as well as socially, a very confusing one. The war had destroyed, or at least seriously challenged, many of the old patterns of American thought. The problem of how to perceive America artistically was a difficult one for many writers. For those who needed it, Mencken structured the American scene in a convenient series of polarities: the individual versus the mass, the elite versus the mob, the artist versus society, rebellion versus conformity, mediocrity versus excellence, and skepticism versus mindless assent. This structure provided some sort of framework for the novelist who might otherwise have been lost amid the chaos of the radically and rapidly changing society around him.

This Menckenized version of America was undoubtedly crippled by the very oversimplifications on which it was based. One must, for example, question the wisdom of insisting that the artist's natural relationship to his society is that of constant rebellion. For the writers who could not give vitality to these ideas, as Lewis did, or who could not eventually go beyond them, as Fitzgerald did in *The Great Gatsby*, Mencken's polarities could prove a trap, not a liberation. But for those with talent and imagination, Mencken did provide a starting point: he gave a writer the means for dealing creatively with the postwar American experience.

Mencken also played an important role in helping the writer to understand his craft and to see it in terms of a wider literary background. Today the would-be author may avail himself of creative writing classes and courses in contemporary literature. As late as the 1920s, however, university courses in American literature and modern writing were rare. It was quite possible for a college graduate to know more about Edward Taylor than about Walt Whitman or even more about Oliver Goldsmith than about George Bernard Shaw. Mencken's essays introduced writers to figures like Nietzsche, Shaw, Conrad, Ibsen, Dreiser, and Mark Twain. It was through Mencken, for example, that Fitzgerald came into contact with Conrad's novels, which, according to the author himself, helped him tighten his form and style, thus making *The Great Gatsby* such a significant advance over his earlier novels.[16]

The legacy that Mencken left the writers of the 1920s was a mixed blessing of insight combined with shallowness, that was at once broadening and limiting. Many of his critics have insisted that he should share the blame for some of the intellectual confusion evident in much of the decade's writing. But when one recalls that the decade witnessed a great blossoming of the American novel, it seems only fair that Mencken should also receive some of the credit for this achievement.

## IV    A Farewell to Art

It is ironic that Mencken achieved his greatest reputation as a critic at the very time that he began thinking of abandoning the arts. As early as 1920 he told Burton Rascoe, "I'll write very little about books hereafter. All my criticism is, at bottom, a criticism of ideas, not of mere books." To poet Louis Untermeyer, Mencken was a bit clearer about the nature of his restlessness. "You will escape from literary criticism, too, as I am trying to do. . . . We live, not in a literary age, but a fiercely political age."[17] In order to understand this shift in Mencken's center of focus, one must recall that his early ideas on criticism were based on a belief that art could be a medium for intellectual change and even for social progress through the work of the artist-iconoclast. Gradually, however, Mencken's faith in the social role of art began to waver, as can be seen in his changing attitude toward his early iconoclastic heroes: Shaw, Ibsen, and Nietzsche.

Shaw had been one of Mencken's earliest idols and the subject of his first book. But by 1916 he had dismissed the Irish playwright as "an orthodox Scotch Presbyterian of the most cock-sure and bilious sort." Shaw the iconoclast was not the "Ulster Polonius."[18] Mencken's reaction against Ibsen was less personal; but he nevertheless denied in 1917 that Ibsen had ever been anything more than a great dramatic craftsman. Ignoring the fact that he himself had once viewed *A Doll's House* as an intellectual breakthrough in drama, Mencken now laughed at those who saw Ibsen as an iconoclast. His ideas were merely "banal."[19] Even Nietzsche was now revealed as a man whose basic ideas might have occurred to "any reasonable *Privat Dozent*." In terms of personality, Mencken claimed that the philosopher stood "a good deal nearer to the average Y.M.C.A. secretary than to Ludendorff."[20]

Had Mencken done no more than attack his former heroes, one might conclude, as have some of his critics, that he was merely demoting his mentors in order to enhance his own stature.[21] However, behind his comments on Shaw, Ibsen, and Nietzsche lay a general abandonment of the idea that art could be a means for intellectual and social change. For example, although Mencken had once been enthusiastic about the theater of ideas as a vehicle for iconoclastic assaults on society's sacred cows, he insisted in the *Smart Set* for November 1921 that "ideas have no more place in drama than they have in music" (142). The following year, in *Prejudices: Third Series,* he dismissed the drama as being the most democratic of art forms—as mere "show for the mob." "The phrase 'drama of ideas' thus becomes a mere phrase. What is actually meant by it is 'drama of platitudes' " (300).

Mencken's disillusionment was not limited to drama. In May 1920, he announced in the *Smart Set* that "A work of art with ideas in it is as sorry a monster as a pretty girl full of Latin. The aim of a work of art is not to make one think painfully, but to make one think beautifully" (139). In an essay about novelist James Branch Cabell, Mencken insisted that the artist's real aim was "not to suggest improvements in the life about him; it is to escape that life altogether."[22] Mencken even became skeptical about the value of truth seeking. "Nine times out of ten, in the arts as in life, there is actually no truth to be discovered; there is only error to be exposed."[23]

Mencken's final break with literature was consumated in a significant manner. By the early 1920s he was becoming impatient with the idea that the critic existed in the shadow of the artist and his works. In "Criticism of Criticism of Criticism," in the first book of *Prejudices,* he had suggested that the proper role of the critic was that of a catalyst: "He makes the work of art live for the spectator; he makes the spectator live for the work of art. Out of the process comes understanding, appreciation, intelligent enjoyment—and that is precisely what the artist tried to produce" (21). In *Prejudices: Third Series,* Mencken proceeded to destroy his own catalyst theory. In "A Footnote on Criticism," he now stated that the superior critic was always swallowed up by the creative artist that dwelled within him. Such a critic "moves inevitably from the work of art to life itself, and begins to take on a dignity that he formerly lacked" (87).

When this happened, the critic "usually ends by abandoning the criticism of specific works of art altogether, and [sets] up shop as a general merchant in general ideas, *i.e.*, as an artist working in the materials of life itself" (88). In Mencken's case the literary critic turned social critic.

Bit by bit Mencken had broken the back of his career and turned away from his whole concept of the interconnection between art and society. This concept had finally given way at its weakest point. Mencken had always assumed that a causal connection existed between the artist and progress, but he never really established the nature of that connection. Almost as an act of faith, he had believed that the iconoclastic power of art would somehow alter public opinion by challenging old ideas and institutions. Events shook that faith; for, in Mencken's point of view, America had moved from the emotional, democratic excesses of Progressivism to the repressive outrages of war-generated hysteria. After the war the quality of art had indeed improved, but American society seemed less enlightened than ever before. Either art had failed or it could accomplish nothing. Mencken had always tried to maintain a dual and contradictory attitude toward art: on the one hand, it was to lead society to reevaluate its basic ideas, but on the other hand, the artist could not allow any ideology that might direct or shape that reevaluation to intrude into his work. The social and the esthetic sides of art had not really been integrated in Mencken's thought. Now, in the 1920s, art, for Mencken, was reduced to only an esthetic role. And since Mencken was primarily interested in society, he bid farewell to art.

## V  *Founding the* Mercury

As a vehicle for the launching of his new career as a social critic, Mencken wanted a new magazine. Both he and his partner Nathan had been dreaming of a periodical of their own ever since the days when they had collaborated with Wright in trying to revamp the *Smart Set*. The model, at least in Mencken's mind, was drawn from H. G. Well's novel, *The New Machiavelli*, first published in 1910. Mencken admired the aristocratic views of Well's hero in the novel who was an elitist seeking to graft scientific Socialism onto British Toryism. The fictional editor's magazine, the *Blue Weekly*, was, in Well's words, to "express and elaborate these conceptions of a new, severer, aristocratic culture"—to make "bold, clever ideas prevail."[24] When Mencken and Nathan began negotiating with Alfred Knopf for the establishment of their new magazine in the early

1920s the name *Blue Review* was the first one suggested; but it was eventually rejected in favor of *The American Mercury*.[25]

The *Mercury* was not merely the product of Mencken's dissatisfaction with the *Smart Set's* low budget and its vaguely tarnished reputation. Mencken wanted a magazine free from literature so that he could embrace the wider world of society and politics. Writing to the idiosyncratic Socialist Upton Sinclair in 1923, Mencken described his hopes for the *Mercury:* "In politics it will be, in the main, Tory, but *civilized* Tory. You know me well enough to know that there will be no quarter for the degraded cads who now run the country. I am against you and against the Liberals because I believe you chase butterflies, but I am even more against your enemies."[26]

It was Mencken's firm belief that many intelligent Americans were opposed to the forces of mediocrity and materialism that seemed to dominate the country in the prosperous decade after the war, and he made his appeal to this audience in the *Mercury's* first editorial of January 1924: "There is no middle ground of consolation for men who believe neither in the Socialist fol-de-rol nor in the principal enemies of the Socialist fol-de-rol—and yet it must be obvious that such men constitute the most intelligent and valuable body of citizens that the nation can boast. . . . It will be the design of *The American Mercury* to bring, if not alleviation of their lot, then at least some solace to these outcasts of democracy." The sort of reader the magazine sought was, in Mencken's words, what "William Graham Sumner called the Forgotten Man—that is, the normal, educated, well-disposed, unfrenzied, enlightened citizen of the middle minority."(28).

Although the editorial was supposed to speak for both Mencken and Nathan, it soon became clear that there were serious disagreements between the editors as to the real nature and purpose of the *Mercury* venture. Nathan, who could not appreciate fully his partner's growing preoccupation with politics, remained dedicated to the arts, particularly to the theater, and viewed politics as merely an inferior form of vaudeville. Moreover, Nathan refused to accept the new note of seriousness that characterized Mencken's involvement with the magazine. He once wrote, "a magazine, to me—and to my associate, friend, and partner Mencken no less—is a toy, something with which to amuse ourselves."[27]

Mencken, however, was not toying with the *Mercury*. Nor was he satisfied with Nathan's attempt to balance the magazine's social and political orientation with literary material that, although often high in artistic quality, was also weak in social relevance. Mencken wanted to be free to follow through with the promise, made in the first editorial, that the *Mercury* would "attempt a realistic presentation of the whole gaudy, gorgeous American scene" (30). Moreover, Mencken was becoming dissastisfied with the editorial arrangements. He had tried to continue the pattern, established in the *Smart Set* days, which left the running of the New York editorial office in Nathan's hands while he worked in Baltimore and made brief journeys to New York to help settle each issue. Mencken was soon complaining that Nathan was not carrying the fair share of the editorial burden.

By October 1924, Mencken had had enough of editorial quarrels. In a long letter to Nathan he unburdened himself of his discontent and pointed to the real issues that divided them. The *Mercury*, he complained, was too casual and trivial; it lacked "solid dignity and influence." "Our interests," he wrote, "are too far apart. We see the world in wholly different colors." The problem had not arisen with the *Smart Set*, "for neither of us took the magazine very seriously." But the *Mercury* was a different matter: "What the magazine needs is a sounder underpinning. It must develop a more coherent body of doctrine, and maintain it with more vigor. It must seek to lead, not a miscellaneous and frivolous rabble, but the class that is serious at bottom, however much it may mock conventional seriousness." Mencken saw great significance in the fact that one of the most successful articles they had published had been an attack on President Coolidge; for "It proves that the civilized minority, after all, does take politics seriously." He believed that the *Mercury* could achieve as solid a position among periodicals as that once occupied by the *Atlantic Monthly*. "Its chances are not unlike those which confronted the Atlantic in the years directly after the Civil War: it has an opportunity to seize leadership of the genuine civilized minority of Americans."[28]

Mencken, as senior editor, insisted that the partnership be dissolved. Knopf, the publisher, who had originally offered the editor's chair to Mencken alone, backed him. By January 1925, the *Mercury* was completely in Mencken's hands. Nathan, now relegated to a desk in the typing pool, continued to contribute the theater reviews and his column "Clinical Notes." But the voice of the *Mercury* was primarily that of H. L. Mencken.

CHAPTER 7

# The Social Critic in the 1920s

E DMUND Wilson, when writing for the *New Republic* in 1921, suggested that Mencken had emerged from World War I with a new seriousness that belied the comic mask of his satire. Mencken, who was usually impatient with such interpretations of his motives, confided to Wilson that "you have there told the truth. The brewery celler, in these days, is as impossible as the ivory tower. For a while the show is simply farce, but inevitably every man feels an irresistible impulse to rush out and crack a head—in other words, to do something positive for common decency."[1]

Mencken had already returned to the *Evening Sun* in Baltimore with a new series of weekly articles that dealt primarily with national issues and that were to run from February 9, 1920, until 1938. By the time the *American Mercury* was launched in 1924, Mencken was a nationally known figure. His books and a series of weekly syndicated articles for the Chicago *Sunday Tribune* helped to extend his reputation.[2] The 1920s mark the apogee of Mencken's popularity, and his success during this decade was the result of the happy conjunction of a man's talent with his times. Mencken's brand of satire—boisterous iconoclasm coupled with a bemused aloofness— had not been tolerated during the war and would not prove popular in the crisis years of the 1930s and early 1940s.

The post–World War I decade, however, presented Mencken with an unique opportunity: peace and prosperity had produced an atmosphere in which confidence was papered on top of confusion and conflict. With the fragmentation of Progressivism and with the ascendancy of retrenchment under the Republicans, politics entered a difficult period of transition. There was also sharp competition between the social, ethnic, and regional groups that were seeking cultural influence, as well as political and economic power. The new economics of consumership and the impact of technological

96

innovations, such as the automobile, the motion picture, and the radio, produced a cultural environment in which traditional values were undermined and in which new problems were only dimly perceived. Amid such confusion, Mencken found wide latitude and many targets for his satire. The show was good, but Mencken was more than a gleeful ringmaster. As he told Edmund Wilson, he intended to crack a skull or two for common decency.

## I  *Civil Liberties*

The suppression of civil liberties was one of the first problems to attract Mencken's attention. Even before the war, he had been sensitive about the threats against individual rights and free speech. During the war, he had been appalled at the wholesale violation of even the most basic constitutional rights. The Red Scare of 1919–1920 and the continuing crackdown by federal and state agencies against radicals and dissenters convinced Mencken that the civil liberties of Americans were endangered. In his first article for the new series in the *Sun* he denounced Attorney General A. Mitchell Palmer, the architect of the Red Scare, for his "medieval attempts to get into the White House by pumping up the Bolshevik issue." "He has probably done more than any other man, save only Mr. Wilson himself, to break down democratic self-government in America and substitute a Cossack despotism, unintelligent and dishonest" (February 9, 1920).[3] Mencken was convinced that one of the major issues in the coming presidential campaign would be personal freedom.

Mencken maintained his running fire against the Justice department throughout most of the decade. He claimed on September 27, 1920, that under Palmer it had deliberately manufactured evidence and so constituted "a conspiracy against justice, and what is more, against common honesty and common decency." Criticizing the deportation of radicals following the Red Scare on April 25, 1921, Mencken held that "Probably two-thirds of those allegedly Reds were wholly innocent, and even the guilty ones were not fairly tried." In *Notes On Democracy*, published in 1926, he accused the Department of Justice of having "resorted to perjury in its efforts to undo men guilty of flouting it, and at all times it has labored valiantly to nullify the guarantees of the Bill of Rights" (183).

Mencken was equally critical of the federal courts for having, in his eyes, concurred in the abrogation of civil liberties. Commenting on the late chief justice of the Supreme Court, Edward D. White, he argued on May 23, 1921, that under White, the Court had reached "depths of supineness never before touched in American History. . . . The net effect of its so-powerful cogitation, during the last few years of his service, has been to upset and make a mock of three out of four of the historic rights and liberties of the American citizens. . . ." He even accused the Supreme Court of failing to maintain the right to trial by jury. Referring to various rulings that upheld laws that removed certain types of cases involving radicals and Prohibition offenders from juries, Mencken alleged on September 15, 1924, that "The whole system of Federal courts is now engaged . . . upon a deliberate and successful effort to blow [trial by jury] to pieces . . . ."

The situation in the individual states was sometimes even worse. Mencken frequently attacked California in particular for its combination of rigid antisyndicalist laws with a notorious bias in its courts against accused radicals. "Only in California is it normal for innocent men to be railroaded to prison on perjured testimony, and for public prosecutors to traffic openly with professional perjurers, training them in their lies . . ." (June 19, 1922). As will be seen in Chapter 9, he did his best to focus attention on the Mooney case, as well as on the Sacco and Vanzetti trials.

Mencken's interest in civil liberties was based on his strong commitment to individual freedom and on his experience with wartime suppression of opinion. Since his involvement certainly did not spring from any left-wing proclivities, his championing of the rights of radicals became all the more meaningful. Part of Mencken's value as a social critic was that he could see beyond his own political and economic beliefs and could judge a problem on principle rather than on ideology. Nowhere is this capability clearer than in his comments about the relationship between capital and labor.

## II   Marx of the Master Class

Mencken clearly believed that the suppression of radicalism, which had started during the war, was the direct result of business pressure on government. It was "physically dangerous," he insisted on October 15, 1923, for a man to so much as hint that a non-capitalistic system would please him. Since Mencken continually called attention to areas where he felt that justice had become tainted by economics, he attacked the frequent use of court injunctions to break strikes. In the scramble for such injunctions against union activity, Mencken saw "mill owners eager to get rid of annoying labor leaders, coal operators bent on making slaves of their miners, and so on. The injunction in strike cases has been a stench for years. . . ."

Similarly, a Supreme Court ruling against labor's use of the secondary boycott against employers brought forth Mencken's satirical observation on January 17, 1921, that it was "the noblest victory that capitalism has won since the celebrated decison against the child labor laws." The doctrines that the Supreme Court seemed to be following were not those set down by the Founding Fathers "but the doctrine of its current Capitalistic masters. . . . It puts maintenance of the *status quo* above everything else . . ." (May 23, 1921). To Mencken, the behavior of the courts was evidence that America was governed "under democratic forms, by a capitalistic oligarchy, and it is so securely in power that no conceivable revolt is likely to prevail against it" (September 24, 1923). Satirically, he announced that the country was approaching a businessman's Utopia: "Nowhere else in the world, . . . is there such elaborate machinery for inoculating the proletariat with safe ideas. Every agency of public information, . . . is rididly controlled, and every agency of counter-propaganda is under a legal ban. The results are visible in two familiar phenomena of the past few years: the complete collapse of organized radicalism, . . . and the successful organization of such societies as the American Legion and the Ku Klux Klan into engines of repression."[4]

Mencken rejected as laughable the idea that the "New Era" had erased the conflict between capital and labor. In the *American Mercury* of March 1929, he claimed that America's economic system was "inordinately wasteful and inhuman. Labor is still frankly a commodity, like iron and coal" (380). Where organized labor survived, it did so, Mencken insisted on February 9, 1925, because its leaders cooperated with the bosses. His example, rather unfairly, was the conservative unionism of Samuel Gompers, the head of the American Federation of Labor. "Where else in the world is there a great union organization that has so long and honorable a record as a strike-breaker? . . . Practically considered, it [the A. F. of L]is not a labor organization at all: it is simply a balloon mattress interposed between capital and labor to protect the former from the latter."

Considering the times and Mencken's own unswerving adherence to capitalism, his scattered but trenchant comments on the position of the working class in America are surprisingly perceptive. Recognizing that the workers had accepted unquestioningly the precepts of the American Dream, which promised economic success in return for hard work, Mencken asserted that "The truth is, perhaps, that nine-tenths of them [the workers] find it almost impossible to think of themselves as workingmen, doomed to labor all their lives; in their secret communion with themselves they still think of themselves as potential capitalists" (September 24, 1923). As a result of this dream, America had never developed a true proletariat. "Instead it has simply developed two bourgeoisies, an upper and a lower. Both are narrow, selfish, corrupt, timorous, docile and ignoble . . ." (November 29, 1920).

How was it that Mencken, economic conservative and elitist, could produce a quasi-radical reading of the relationship between government, business, and labor in America? Mencken shared one thing in common with the Marxist analysts: he saw American society in terms of conflict rather than consensus. He was a bit shrewder than most Marxists, however, because he recognized that conflict in America was cultural as well as economic. In the end, of course, Mencken's own loyalties lay with the middle class and not with the plutocracy or with the working class. The last thing he wanted was a triumph of radicalism, but he was also convinced that unprincipled suppression of the left was itself a guarantee of the creation for more radicalism. After having urged rejection of Coolidge, he wrote, on October 6, 1924, "I contend that it [the president's reelection] is bound to manufacture radicalism in a wholesale manner, and that this radicalism will be far more dangerous to legitimate business than the mild stuff that Dr. La Follette [Coolidge's opponent] now has on tap." The problem of the violations of the rights of labor activists and of radicals may also be seen as part of another area of concern that interested Mencken: the growth of governmental power and the misuse of law in American society. The key issue in this context, however, was Prohibition.

### III  *Law And Order In a Dry Decade*

Mencken, who made no fetish of law and order, once defined the American concept of law and order as meaning "harsh laws, unintelligently administered." For him there were either good laws or bad laws. Since bad laws subverted good order, Americans, he insisted, had to choose between law and order. To do so, citizens had to fight laws that threatened their liberties. "Such laws deserve no respect, and deserving no respect, they deserve no obedience." Far from being a criminal, the violator of such laws "is worthy of admiration and imitation" (February 26, 1923). Commenting in *Prejudices: Fifth Series* on legislation that prohibited people from speaking on behalf of birth control, Mencken stormed: "The way to dispose of such laws is to flout them and make a mock of them. The theory that they can be got rid of by enforcing them is nonsense. Enforcing them simply inspires the sadists who advocate them to fresh excesses. Worse, it accustoms the people to oppression, and so tends to make them bear it uncomplainingly. . . . No, the way to deal with such laws is to defy them and thus make them ridiculous" (14). True to his word, when the *American Mercury* was banned in Boston in 1926, Mencken personally went to that city, sold copies of the offending issue, and was arrested, tried, and acquitted.[5]

The "bad" law that most often concerned Mencken was the Volstead Act, which had been passed in 1919 to enforce the Prohibition Amendment to the Constitution. The Eighteenth Amendment prohibited the manufacture, sale, or transportation of intoxicating liquors. The Volstead Act, which assigned Prohibition enforcement to the Bureau of Internal Revenue, defined "intoxicating liquors" as any beverage containing from one-half to one percent of alcohol—a ban which, strictly applied, could have driven sauerkraut from the market.

Viewed at the distance of a half-century, the gap between Mencken's rhetorical defense of individual liberties and the actual threat offered by Prohibition may seem too vast for serious contemplation. Americans needed no ringing appeals to assert the rights of man in order to send them out in search of a bootlegger. But, while it is true that Mencken was obsessed with Prohibition, his obsession was at least partially justified. As Richard Hofstadter once noted, Prohibition sometimes seems like "a historical detour, a meaningless nuisance, an extraneous imposition upon the main course of history. . . ." Yet, as Hofstadter also indicated, Prohibition was indeed *the* major issue of the 1920s,[6] which not only seriously affected the nation's politics but was the focal point for various pressures that were building up within the society. As a sincere, if poorly conceived reform, Prohibition marked the high tide of both certain Progressive theories of human engineering and the involvement of evangelical Protestantism in social problems.[7] Simultaneously, it became a battle ground for various groups and philosophies that were competing for control of American culture: middle class versus working class, native-born Americans versus immigrant, country versus town, old Progressivism versus new liberalism. Prohibition raised vital questions concerning such issues as governmental power, the proper role of police and government agents, the sanctity of privacy, cultural pluralism, and public morality. It is hardly surprising that Mencken regarded Prohibition as a symbol of the nation's ills.

Appreciative of alcohol in most of its potable forms (he once described himself as being "ombibulous"), Mencken was also too prejudiced against any attempts to legislate morals to deal fairly with so complex an issue as Prohibition. On September 3, 1928, he claimed that "the whole 'moral' movement in the United States has been in partnership with political corruption." In *Notes On Democracy* he charged that the Volstead Act "destroys the constitutional right to a jury trial, and in its administration the constitutional prohibition of unreasonable search and seizures and the rule against double jeopardy are habitually violated" (168).

Although too biased to even contemplate the dry side of the argument, Mencken did try to focus public attention upon some of the political and social principles involved. Yet as Americans went about their pragmatic way of procuring illegal booze, Mencken occasionally despaired of rousing libertarian protests. "Even the popular discontent with Prohibition," he lamented in the *Mercury* in May 1926, "is not a discontent with its sneaking and knavishness—its wholesale turning loose of licensed blacklegs and blackmailers, its degradation of the judiciary, its corruption of Congress, its disingenuous invasion of the Bill of Rights. . . . Of any forthright grappling with the underlying indecency there is little show" (35).

## IV  *The Husbandman*

Prohibition was so central an issue in Mencken's social criticism during the decade because he sensed in it a double threat. On the one hand, it disturbed his libertarian sensibilities; on the other, he perceived it as part of a larger cultural struggle between the countryside and the cities. "What lies under it [Prohibition], and under all the other crazy enactments of its category," he complained in *Prejudices: Fourth Series,* "is no more and no less than the yokel's congenital and incurable hatred of the city man . . . "(54). Tension between city and countryside is common to most societies and a factor endemic in American history, hardly unique to the 1920s. By the beginning of the decade, however, events had thrown the differences between the urban and rural areas into unusually sharp relief. Industrialization and immigration, which characterized the urbanizing process in America, had produced a cultural environment in the cities that was markedly different from that of the countryside. Urban prosperity and rural depression in the decade helped accentuate this difference. Finally, postwar advances in the mass media and in transportation had brought Americans into closer contact with one another. Instead of increased unity, however, familiarity bred an increased contempt between city man and country cousin.

Mencken took it upon himself to champion the cause of the "beleaguered" cities against the "barbaric yokels" from the hinterland. In a total repudiation of the agrarian myth, Mencken focused his most scathing satire on the image of the farmer. "No more grasping, selfish and dishonest mammal, indeed, is known to students of the Anthropoidea," he wrote in *Prejudices: Fourth Series*. "When the going is good for him he robs the rest of us up to the extreme limit of our endurance; when the going is bad he comes bawling for help out of the public till" (46). At the same time, political apportionment and the congressional seniority system gave the rural areas a disproportionate share of power, making them "the reservoir of all the nonsensical legislation which now makes the United States a buffoon among the great nations" (54).

Both sides in the urban-rural controversies had their just complaints. However, Mencken's antiagrarianism was so one-sided and so extreme that it can be understood only in terms of his startling ignorance of rural America. Mencken was almost unique among the writers of the decade who criticized rural America in that he was born and bred an East Coast urbanite, who thus lacked that firsthand experience with and even affection for the farms and small towns that create the interesting ambiguity in the writings of Sherwood Anderson, Sinclair Lewis, Edgar Lee Masters, and others. Although Mencken encouraged their work, he was not, strictly speaking, a part of the "Revolt from the Village."[8] For Mencken, rural America was nothing more than an abstraction—a satirical abstraction of all of those forces that he felt were threatening enlightened government and civilized tastes. For this reason, his targets were not so much the small town citizens of Lewis or Anderson but the less complex and more easily satirized figure of the farmer who lay closest to the heart of American political and social mythology. Significantly, when Mencken published his most vicious antiagrarian essay in *Prejudices: Fourth Series*, he entitled it "The Husbandman," Thomas Jefferson's term for the ideal citizen of the Republic.

## V  *The Fundamentalist Crusade*

One reason for Mencken's hostility to rural America was the association in his mind between agrarian politics and evangelical Protestantism. "Once we get rid of campmeeting rule we'll get rid simultaneously of the Klan, the Anti-Saloon League and the Methodist Board of Temperance, Prohibition and Public Morals." During the presidential campaign of 1928, Mencken believed that the only issues were Prohibition and religion—"or more accurately, only religion, for Prohibition, in the dry areas, has long ceased to be a question of government or even ethics, and has become purely theological" (November 5, 1928).

Evangelical Protestantism was a very active force in America during the Jazz Age. The Fundamentalist Movement, as it was called, had begun prior to the war as a counter-offensive by conservative Protestants against modernist theology. By the middle of the 1920s, Fundamentalism was a large and popular movement, especially in the rural Midwest and South, although it did have its urban adherents. Fundamentalists not only supported moral reforms, such as Prohibition, but also actively lobbied state legislatures for laws against the teaching of the Darwinian theory of evolution, which contradicted the biblical account of Creation. The anti-Darwin crusade, led by William Jennings Bryan, culminated in the famous "Monkey Trial" in Dayton, Tennessee, in 1925. After an antievolutionary law had been passed in that state, a group of Dayton citizens decided to test it. A high school teacher, John T. Scopes, agreed to present the evolutionary theory to his class. His arrest and trial became the most famous court case of a decade that, all too often, saw the ballyhoo of the circus invade the court room.

Although sent to cover the trial by the *Sunpapers*, Mencken was not merely there as a reporter. He was a combatant in what he sincerely took to be a struggle of civilization and science against bigotry and superstition. "Let no one mistake it for comedy, farcical though it may be in all its details," he commented on July 18, 1925, about the trial. "It serves notice on the country that Neanderthal man is organizing in these forlorn backwaters of the land, led by a fanatic [Bryan] rid of sense and devoid of conscience. Tennessee, challenging him too timorously and too late, now sees its courts converted into camp meetings and its Bill of Rights made a mock of by its sworn officers of the law. There are other States that had better look to their arsenals before the Hun is at their gates."

Mencken had been instrumental in urging the famous criminal lawyer and libertarian, Clarence Darrow, to offer his services to the American Civil Liberties Union, which was conducting Scopes's defense. And at several pretrial meetings with Darrow and with the American Civil Liberties Union lawyer Dudley Field Malone, Mencken suggested that the defense so shape its strategy that it discredit Bryan, who was leading the prosecution team.[9] In the end, Bryan was tempted to take the stand as an expert on the Bible and had to endure Darrow's vicious cross-examination. Although the prosecution won at Dayton, Scopes was later acquitted on a technicality. It was an anticlimax to what Mencken had hoped would be a great test case of the Constitution.

As with the case of Prohibition, Mencken was too much of a partisan to appreciate or even recognize that the Fundamentalists' fears, if not necessarily their methods, had a certain legitimacy. The Fundamentalists faced the very difficult problem that arises when public schools teach children doctrines to which their parents are deeply opposed. Moreover, as Paul Carter has indicated, the Dayton trial was not, in fact, the battle between liberty and intolerance that Mencken painted. In presenting the Darwinian thesis, the authors of Scopes's textbook, *Civic Biology*, were in their own way just as dogmatic as Bryan, whose authority rested on the Bible. The unquestioned orthodoxy of the textbook writers, as well as for Darrow and Mencken, was science.[10] There is a certain irony, then, in Mencken's scathing attacks on Bryan, especially in "In Memoriam: W. J. B." in *Prejudices: Fifth Series*. In spite of all the differences between Mencken and Bryan, they both had their orthodoxies, and they both felt uncomfortable with the direction in which postwar America was moving. Bryan fought modernism in terms of education and theology, and Mencken resisted its pressures on the sanctity and the dignity of the individual.

## VI  *The Flight From Babylon*

It would be a mistake to take at face value Mencken's self-conscious identification with the cities. While he turned rural America into a satirical abstraction for what he conceived to be the nation's weaknesses, he made the city into a metaphor for the civilized values that he felt were endangered. Neither the abstraction nor the metaphor were soundly based on reality. For example, Mencken, writing on November 2, 1925, claimed that, "City rights are worth immensely more than State rights. The city is a genuine community; the State is only too often simply a geographical expression." It is very difficult to think of American cities in the 1920s, with their ever-increasing influx of rural migrants (black and white) and their polygot ethnic populations, as communities, especially when one compares the cities with the more homogeneous small towns such as Dayton, Tennessee. Mencken clearly had an ideal concept of the city—an admirable one, but one that was threatened more by the very nature of the American process of urbanization than by the rural pastors and their flocks.

Mencken's involvement in the rural-urban conflict prevented him from making a realistic and honest evaluation of the urban America he sought to defend. Yet he was in fact critical of at least certain aspects of city life. For instance, although dedicated to progress, Mencken was not enthusiastic about the effects of industrialization. In "Libido for the Ugly," in *Prejudices: Sixth Series,* he recounted a train trip through Westmoreland County, an area just east of Pittsburgh, Pennsylvania: "Here was the heart of industrial America, the center of its most lucrative and characteristic activity, the boast and pride of the richest and grandest nation ever seen on earth—and here was a scene so dreadfully hideous, so intolerably bleak and forlorn that it reduced the whole aspiration of man to a macabre and depressing joke" (187). If the industrial landscape was a horror, the industrial cityscape in America was often little better.

The unconscious ambivalence of Mencken's urbanism can also be seen in "On Living in Baltimore," which appeared in *Prejudices: Fifth Series.* The essay is actually a comparison between New York City and Baltimore—a contrast between what Mencken found good and bad in urban life. Explaining why he preferred to live in Baltimore, although his work took him regularly to New York, Mencken claimed that Gotham was fit only "for the gross business of getting money" and not for living. What made New York so dreadful in his eyes was the fact that most of its citizens had no real homes and, therefore, no traditions or sense of community. The average New Yorker was a denizen of flats and apartments: "His quarters are precisely like the quarters of 50,000 other men. The front he presents to the world is simply an anonymous door on a gloomy corridor. Inside, he lives like a sardine in a can. Such habitation, it must be plain, cannot be called a home" (239–40).

What made Baltimore a superior place to live was the strength of its traditions—the rooted feeling it could still impart to its inhabitants. Because its people lived in real homes, they had permanence and stability in their lives. In Baltimore, a man's "contacts are with men and women who are rooted as he is. They are not moving all the time, and so they are not changing their friends all the time. Thus abiding relationships tend to be built up, and when fortune brings unexpected changes, they survive those changes" (242). Although a certain amount of truth existed in Mencken's comparison between Baltimore and New York, rootless mobility was not an exclusively New York phenomenon by the 1920s. By presenting Baltimore as his ideal city, Mencken was praising a personal urban experience that was becoming less and less characteristic of American cities.

Indeed, even Baltimore was not safe from the threat of destructive change. Mencken might happily announce that the charms of his city had survived, "despite the frantic efforts of boosters and boomers who, in late years, have replaced all its ancient cobblestones with asphalt, and bedizened it with Great White Ways and suburban boulevards, and surrounded it with stinking steel plants and oil refineries, and increased its population from 400,000 to 800,000" (237). Nevertheless, the dangers were present, and Mencken recognized them. He was, in fact, no more at home with the reality of urban America than he was with his distorted image of the rural villages and farms of his imagination. In putting forth his urban ideal, he was, like Bryan, defending certain traditional values that were under increasing pressure from a rapidly changing American society.

## VII   *The Admass Society*

There was a great deal of restless anger in Mencken's writings in the decade that could not be contained within the twin themes of libertarianism and the rural-urban conflict. Beneath Mencken's satire one hears a *cri de coeur* raised against the deterioration of the quality of American life. In an article on his home state of Maryland, he lamented the loss of charm and color that had passed with the old tidewater aristocracy. All the links with the past were broken, he complained. "Maryland was once a state of mind; now it is a machine." In the end, he dismally predicted, his state would, like the rest of America, endure a "complete obliteration of distinction, a wiping out of all the old traditions, a massive triumph of regimentation."[11]

The reasons for Mencken's lamentation over Maryland's future become clearer when one considers what T. C. Cochran and William Miller have concluded about the social impact of "New Era" economics: "Under pressure to put the nation's savings to work in productive enterprises, American business men vigorously pushed their sales on automobiles, radios, and moving pictures. And as rapid urbanization and agricultural discontent weakened traditional agrarian individualism, the perfection of these new devices of communications together with the older newspapers and national magazines broke down local insularity. Metropolis and village, city and country, factory town and suburban park came increasingly under identical business influences. Provincial habits and customs crumbled."[12]

What had evolved in the 1920s was America's, and very likely the world's, first admass society. An admass society is one in which popular culture is dominated by national (and eventually international) mass media which are influenced or controlled by large consumer-oriented industries. The mass media, either directly through advertising or indirectly through the consumer-oriented values of its contents, create a continuing desire for products, the ownership of which becomes the primary means of defining not only one's class but even one's personality. The economic propaganda for consumption, which is the prime force in an admass society, is intense, and in the 1920s it was still a relatively new force. As Edward Bernays noted approvingly in 1928, "As civilization has become more complex, the technical means have been invented and developed by which opinion may be regimented."[13]

Mencken's understanding of the new admass society was rather like the blindman's perception of the elephant: he grasped some of its attributes, but he could never really define the whole. The basis for his social analysis, such as it was, rested on people and principles and not upon the impersonal forces of economics and technological change. Nevertheless, it is against this backdrop of the emerging admass society that Mencken's never-ending stream of satire aimed at the George F. Babbits and Calvin Coolidges must be seen. Richard Hofstadter noted that whereas business men in the Progressive Era had been criticized for their economic and political actions, they were ridiculed in the 1920s for their cultural shortcomings: "Where once he had been speculator, exploiter, corrupter and tyrant, he had now become boob and philistine, prude and conformist . . . ."[14] The tone of such criticism was often snobbish, and Mencken certainly was prepared to indict a Babbitt for being ignorant of Beethoven or a Coolidge for not reading Hauptmann. But the antibusiness sentiment of the decade went much deeper than such self-gratifying elitist exercises. When Mencken complained on February 9, 1925, that "The United States, I believe, is the first great nation in history of the world to ground its whole national philosophy upon business," he was attacking much more than Philistinism. For, as he indicated on June 22, 1925, "Business is not an end in itself; it is simply a means. Its object is to supply the needs of human beings, not to make slaves of them. . . . [Business] is not the supreme aim of human existence on this earth, and any doctrine that so regards it is ignorant and pernicious."

Mencken's attacks on what James Truslow Adams called "Our Business Civilization" went beyond intellectual snobbery. He was reacting to the immense pressures upon the individual and upon the community that were created by the new economic order. By personifying the enemy in terms of the businessman and the politician, Mencken contributed little to the understanding of the underlying forces that were shaping the admass society. But he was eloquent in expressing his anger at the increased conformity and regimentation in American life. As he wrote in the *Mercury* in July 1927, the free man in modern America was being turned into a "Freudian case." "Every one of us has been under the steam-roller; every one of us, in this way or that, conforms unwillingly, and has the corpse of a good impulse below stairs" (290).

Certainly, the analytical basis of Mencken's social criticism was often weak. Founded upon an amalgamation of Social Darwinism and Nietzsche, Mencken tended to see everything in terms of polarities: ignorance versus enlightenment, corruption versus honesty, injustice versus decency, and the mob versus the individual. These polarities provided much of the punch of his satire, but his approach was too simplistic a one to enable him to grasp all of the complexities of the age he sought to criticize. Yet Mencken was able, in a rough way, to point up some of the important questions of the decade; and, in focusing on conflict rather than upon consensus, he offers to the student of the 1920s some genuine insights into the nature of the period.

For his own age, Mencken's value lay in the passionate indignation with which he exposed the many threats to America's social and even moral values. He was, as Eric Goldman has suggested, a latter-day Muckraker, whose theme was the "shame of the Babbitts."[15] A critic with a stronger ideological awareness of America's problems might have dug much deeper into the injustices of the society during the 1920s, but few would have been more eloquent than was Mencken in stating their principles. He firmly believed, as he wrote in *Prejudices: Sixth Series,* that "the first aim of civilization is to augment and safeguard the dignity of man—that it is worth nothing to be a citizen of a commonwealth which holds the humblest citizen cheaply and uses him ill" (77).

## VIII   *The Other America*

Mencken extended his criticism of American life beyond the boundaries of essays and articles, but his role as a magazine editor put the capstone of uniqueness upon his career during the 1920s. For the *American Mercury, his* magazine in every sense of the word, mirrored his passions and prejudices; and no other quality periodical was as scathing and as all-pervasive in its criticism of America. If a contribution somehow lacked the necessary bite, the editor was not opposed to sprinkling it with Menckenisms; indeed, half of the magazine's contents sometimes read as if they had come from Mencken's typewriter.[16]

The *Mercury* even carried a special department entitled "Americana" that was made up of examples of the inanities of American life as gleaned from the nation's press. One typical piece was an extract from a speech given by a president of the University of Arizona: "We cannot accept European music as the basis of our music, because it is founded on monarchical and aristocratic notions." The cumulative effect of the "Americana" department alone seemed to justify the sentiments that Mencken once expressed in his famous catechism: "*Q.* If you find so much that is unworthy of reverence in the United States, then why do you live here? A. Why do men go to zoos?"

As Frederick Hoffman has noted with some justice, "As comedy, the gestures transcribed from life in 'Americana' mark the worst form of social and intellectual error of which a democratic people are capable. They are grotesque extremes." Extending his criticism to Mencken himself, Hoffman argues that the editor's picture of his country was "a gigantic parody of the social metaphor." While Mencken "never lied; he never actually told the truth."[17] Hoffman, however, missed two important points. First, Mencken was a satirist, and satire distorts. Second, Mencken's portrait of America as it appeared in the *Mercury* was not, in fact, executed as a monochrome of hostility and jeering rejection. His mind still juggled with two unresolved, conflicting images of America. This dualism is clearly evident in his magazine. The public was entertained (and outraged) by his continual depiction of America as an oppressive "zoo." On the other hand, Mencken and the *Mercury* also fully explored another America that was dynamic, exciting, and full of hidden variety—an America in which some values still retained their resilience.

In the December 1928, editorial that marked the *Mercury*'s fifth anniversary, Mencken himself claimed that the business of setting forth the absurdities of American life was one of the least of the *Mercury*'s concerns. "It has given a great deal more space to something quite different, namely, to introduce one kind of American to another" (408). What Mencken had in mind were the many articles about urban immigrant groups, often written by children of the ghettos; excellent pieces on blacks written by blacks; autobiographical experiences from Americans of dozens of walks of life. A full roster of *Mercury* contributors would include hobos, prison inmates, bricklayers, coal-crackers, dock-wallopers, lawyers, generals, Indians, prostitutes, and even a United States senator.

Moreover, Mencken tried to penetrate beneath the surface of the standardized admass society in order to focus on regional variety. He ran a series of articles on the regional press, on local poets, and on the individual states themselves. Of the eleven states in which ten or more *Mercury* contributors were born, eight were midwestern and southern states. Of the ten in which ten or more *Mercury* writers lived, six were west of the Monongahela and south of the Mason-Dixon line.[18] As Mencken stated in the fifth anniversary editorial of the *Mercury*, December 1928: "Despite the ironing-out process, life in America continues to be infinitely various. There are thousands of back-waters that remain to be explored. There are many adventures that have yet to find their bards" (409). The *Mercury*, he claimed, had tried to survey life in America from "visionaries to criminals, from heroes to poor fish. But all of them, writing out of their own lives, have written with that earnest simplicity which is beyond all art. . ." (408).

The magazine also explored the American past. Although the term "debunking" is often associated with Mencken, neither he nor his magazine often submitted American historical figures to the superficial iconoclasm popular during the decade. Myths and legends but not real men suffered at the hands of contributors such as Charles Beard, Bernard De Voto, William E. Dodd, and Louis M. Hacker. The literary past also received sympathetic and responsible attention in essays about writers who had hitherto been neglected, such as Poe, Crane, Melville, and especially Whitman.[19] Mencken also devoted a good deal of attention to that part of the American past in which he himself was rooted. The 1880s and 1890s came alive with articles on the old-time saloons, horse cars, vaudeville, traveling medicine shows, and circuses. Mencken's purpose was to contrast the old, vital America that was passing with the plastic age that had come into being. As he noted in a review of Thomas Beer's *The Mauve Decade* in the *Mercury* of July 1926, "The Americano no longer dances gorgeously with arms and legs. He has become civilized, which is to say, he has joined a country club. His father roared in the stews and saloons" (383).

Mencken no doubt exaggerated when he claimed that "An idea is represented in *The American Mercury* which is wholly new and significant. Through its influence America has been completely rediscovered, from flora and fauna to the inevitable Indians."[20] Nonetheless, this sentiment accurately reflects the reverse side of the *Mercury*'s satirical criticism of America, for it suggests his own commitment to that *other* America that he loved. For Mencken could defend as well as attack. His criticisms of conformity and his emphasis on diversity called attention to what was endangered by the new forces in American society that he himself only partially understood. If he was often grossly unfair and uninformed in his satiric tirades against the boobs and Babbitts, it was because he saw them as the betrayers of a better America that, for all its faults, was still admirable, still worth defending.

CHAPTER 8

# Democracy and Character

THE day-to-day rough and tumble of American politics was the delight of Mencken's life. He followed the maneuverings of politicians in the newspapers and in the *Congressional Record* as other men followed baseball standings or the stock market reports. When the summer solstice rolled around on the American presidential leap year, he put aside his personal problems and whatever minor ills that gnawed at his hyprochondria and packed his bags for the party conventions. Nothing could keep him away. Nothing could dampen his enthusiasm. Returning from the Coughlin-Townsend convention in 1936, he told Jim Tully that "There were moments when I almost blew up with delight."[1] What small boys found in circuses and grown women in opera Mencken found in American politics; for no other art form so successfully combined farce with high drama. Mencken has often been criticized for propagating the cynical view of politics as a "carnival of buncombe" (although there is as yet no hard, empirical evidence to suggest that this definition of politics is totally inapplicable). Yet underneath the burlesque, Mencken did take politics seriously. In his articles, he discussed issues and candidates and seldom failed to champion some presidential hopeful. And he always voted.[2]

## I  Notes On Democracy

Judging from Mencken's daily involvement with politics on the journalistic level and his long-held dissents from the clichés of American democracy, *Notes On Democracy* (1926) should have been his best book. Its writing had been on his mind since the beginning of the 1920s; but unfortunately, the pressure of his work and the totally subjective passion that he brought to his subject produced a weak pastiche of ideas, enlivened only by a series of well-written satirical set pieces. Reviewing the book in the *Saturday Review of*

*Literature* in December 11, 1926, Walter Lippmann considered *Notes on Democracy* to be in one sense, "a collection of trite and somewhat confused ideas. To discuss it as one might discuss ideas of a first-rate thinker . . . would be to destroy the book and miss its importance" (413).

Before considering Lippmann's qualification to this otherwise damning statement, one must first understand the failure of *Notes on Democracy* as a *political* work; for in it Mencken does nothing more than follow his well-established pattern of satiric criticism— the inversion of the national myths. "The truth is," he wrote, "that the common man's love of liberty, like his love of sense, justice and truth, is almost wholly imaginary. As I have argued, he is not actually happy when free; he is uncomfortable, a bit alarmed, and intolerably lonely. He longs for the warm, reassuring smell of the herd, and is willing to take the herdsman with it" (147). Far from liberating men, Mencken argued that democracy created a tyranny of the mediocre majority over society's intellectual elite. The superior individual, he insisted, "is the chief victim of the democratic process. It not only tries to regulate his acts; it also tries to delimit his thoughts. . . ." The aim of democracy was to break all free spirits "to the common harness" (150–51).

*Notes on Democracy,* then, is simply a continuation of Mencken's "prejudices," a reiteration of his Nietzschean view that society was essentially the battle ground between the superior man and the mob. It is not the polemic that surprises, however, but the almost total disinclination on Mencken's part to base his arguments on anything remotely resembling political or social analysis. His very manner of approaching the problem of democratic society made any such analysis impossible, as can be seen in the following passage. "The free man is one who has won a small and precarious territory from the great mob of his inferiors, and is prepared and ready to defend it and make it support him. All around him are his enemies, and where he stands there is no friend. He can hope for little help from other men of his own kind, for they have battles of their own to fight. He has made of himself a sort of god in his little world, and he must face the responsibilities of a god, and the dreadful loneliness" (45). In such a barren landscape, society itself seems to disappear.

The problem becomes even more serious when one considers Mencken's attitude toward the state. Although any critique of a political system must eventually focus on the institution of the state,

Mencken, throughout all his writings, tended to dismiss the state as, at best, a necessary evil. He asserted in the sixth book of *Prejudices* that "What ails the world mainly, at least in the political sense, is that its governments are too strong. It [government] has been a recurrent pest since the dawn of civilization" (53). In the "Editorial" in the *Mercury* for February 1925, he even managed to see in the wide-spread disobedience of the Volstead Act the "first glimmers of a revolt that must one day shake the world—a revolt, not against this or that form of government, but against the tyranny at the bottom of *all* governments. Government, today, is growing too strong to be safe. There are no longer any citizens in the world; there are only subjects." Almost twenty years later, he mused in some unpublished notes, "I am convinced . . . that government—*any* government—is a nearly unmixed evil, and that abolishing it altogether would be better for mankind than continuing its development along the path now followed."[3] The interest in governmental centralization and in iconoclastic leadership in politics that Mencken had displayed during the Progressive period had dissolved into disillusionment.

Mencken never really looked at the state or at government in institutional terms. It is not surprising, therefore, to find that he devoted very little attention in *Notes on Democracy* to his supposed alternative to democracy: aristocracy. Mencken's aristocracy remained nothing more than an abstract ideal that never cast even the shadow of reality upon American society. Like his view of democracy, it was totally innocent of analysis. *Notes On Democracy*, then, was not a political book in any meaningful sense of the word. If, as Lippmann suggested, the book did have some importance, one must look for its significance in something other than in the realms of political thought.

## II   *The Social Critic as Moralist*

Lippmann thought that *Notes on Democracy* had captured the antidemocratic mood of the times just as Tom Paine's writings had once set forth the late eighteenth century drift toward democracy. Viewing Mencken's book from a different angle, a recent scholar has noted that "There is so much more about Democratic Man than about democracy that this type can be said to be *the* argument of the book. Politics becomes anthropology."[4] Edmund Wilson, seeing *Notes on Democracy* as a prose poem ("the obverse of *Leaves of*

*Grass"*), came closest to perceiving the real focus of the work. Writing in the *New Republic* in December 15, 1926, Wilson saw that Mencken's most important achievement was his portrait of democratic man as "super-boob."

Wilson's point can be illustrated by choosing almost any passage from *Notes on Democracy*. Considering the nature of the average man, Mencken wrote:

He has changed but little since the earliest recorded time, and that change is for the worse quite as often as it is for the better. He still believes in ghosts, and has only shifted his belief in witches to the political sphere. He is still a slave to priests, and trembles before their preposterous magic. He is lazy, improvident and unclean. All the durable values of the world, though his labour has entered into them, have been created against his opposition. He can imagine nothing beautiful and he can grasp nothing true. Whenever he is confronted by a choice between two ideas, the one sound and the other not, he chooses, almost infallibly, and by a sort of pathological compulsion, the one that is not. Behind all the great tyrants and butchers of history he has marched with loud hosannas, but his hand is eternally against those who seek to liberate the spirit of the race. He was in favour of Nero and Torquemada by instinct, and he was against Galileo and Savonarola by the same instinct. When a Cagliostro dies he is ready for a Danton; from the funeral of a Barnum he rushes to the triumph of a Bryan. The world gets nothing from him save his brute labour and even that he tries to evade. It owes nothing to him that has any solid dignity or worth, not even democracy. In two thousand years he has moved an inch: from the sports of the arena to the lynching-party—and another inch: from the obscenities of the Saturnalia to the obscenities of the Methodist revival. So he lives out his life in the image of Jahveh. What is worth knowing he doesn't know and doesn't want to know; what he knows is not true. The cardinal articles of his credo are the inventions of mountebanks; his heroes are mainly scoundrels (64–65).

This creature, as Wilson remarked in his review, is "an ideal monster, exactly like the Yahoo of Swift, and it has almost the same dreadful reality." The world that Mencken depicted in *Notes on Democracy* was "simply an abstraction from *our* world of all those features of American life that fall short of Mr. Mencken's standards" (110).

These standards—Mencken's system of values as applied to human character and society—form the real basis for almost everything he wrote, especially *Notes on Democracy*. In it, Mencken was concerned with what he took to be the failure of character under democracy: "Liberty means self-reliance. It means resolution, it means enterprise, it means the capacity for doing without" (45). The average man lacked these qualities, however, because "Liberty is unfathomable to him. He can no more comprehend it than he can comprehend honour" (46). The basis of Mencken's argument was not political, economic, or sociological; he simply contrasted two types of human character as he imagined them: the one was predisposed toward liberty and the other toward conformity. This concern for character appeared time and again in Mencken's social criticism. In the *Mercury* of January 1929, Mencken commented on the dismissal of economist Scott Nearing from the staff of the University of Pennsylvania for his radical views. Mencken rejected Nearing's Socialism as "hooey," but he greatly admired the man. "What our third-rate snivilization fails to estimate at its real worth is the resolute courage and indomitable devotion of such men. His virtues are completely civilized ones; he is brave, independent, unselfish, urbane and enlightened." If he had a son, Mencken commented, he would want him to meet Nearing. "There is something even more valuable to civilization than wisdom, and that is character. Nearing has it" (124).

Even Mencken's attitude toward political candidates was influenced more by his estimation of their character than of their programs. In the presidential campaign of 1924 he found the candidates of both the Republicans and the Democrats unpalatable, and he therefore turned to the third party candidacy of Robert M. La Follette. La Follette's ideas, Mencken claimed, were so vague as to be incomprehensible; but Mencken voted for him "simply and solely because he was the man of honor among the candidates." He portrayed La Follette's defeat as a joke that the American people had played upon themselves. "Mislead by inflammatory and nonsensical issues, alarmed and run amuck by quacks and montebanks, the people forget the one quality that is worth more in a high officer of state than all the rest. That one quality is character."[5] Mencken followed the same approach in 1928 when he depicted Al Smith as a gentleman from the aristocratic mold: "He is enlightened, he is high-minded, he is upright and trustworthy. What Fredrick the Great said of his officers might well be said of him: he will not lie, and he cannot be bought. Not much more can be said of any man."[6]

In reality, Mencken was a very different figure from the cynical

Nihilist depicted by careless critics of his time and reiterated since then by some equally careless historians. He never denied the importance of values or their necessity in society. He never sought to destroy those values that he believed essential. He did attack, sometimes ignorantly and intolerantly, ideals that seemed to him hypocritical or false. Even then he produced his condemnation by juxtaposing the qualities he admired against those he rejected. Throughout his writings, certain key words constantly reoccur: "dignity," "decency," "honesty," "courage," and, most often, "honor." "Every man has feelings," he once wrote to Fanny Butcher. "Mine chiefly revolve around a concept of honor."[7]

Whatever may be said about Mencken's lack of ability in analyzing political institutions, it should be clear that his interest lay ultimately not with politics but with character and human conduct. Ethics and not ideologies and institutions were his principal concerns. He was in his own way a moralist who busily decried the erosion of those values necessary to a humane and civilized society. Beneath the surface of his satire and social criticism there thundered a constant jeremiad that was delivered to a wayward people who had wandered from the paths of the good and the honorable.

### III   *In Defense of the Forgotten Man*

Mencken could pass off his polemics on character as a critique of democracy because he appeared to champion the virtues of the gentleman and aristocrat against the elemental appetites and fears of the craven, venal mob. Mencken's standard of values was not, however, derived from either a real or an imagined aristocracy. When he hailed the Forgotten Man as his ideal citizen in the first issue of the *American Mercury,* he unwittingly underscored the source of his own code of conduct. As noted earlier, Mencken described the Forgotten Man as "the normal, educated, well-disposed, unfrenzied, enlightened citizen of the middle minority. . . ."—in other words, as an intelligent and responsible member of the middle class. And it was the values of this class that Mencken celebrated and defended. As Douglas C. Stenerson has suggested, ". . . Mencken cultivated the virtues associated with the Protestant ethic, and for him, as frequently as for the Forgotten Man, these virtues had lost all traces of religious feeling. He exhibited and admired in others, individual initiative, hard work, punctuality, thrift and prompt payment of debts. . . ."[8] If one adds honor, dignity, integrity, and character to the list, one is still not very far from the core of traditional American bourgeois values, as a glance at any McGuffey reader will quickly show. Mencken's supposed aristocratic values were formed, not in some remote and romantic Germany of his mind or in the old Maryland tidewater estates, which he never knew, but in the middle class, whose loyal if sometimes errant and eccentric son he remained.

Mencken's defense of middle class values through the image of the Forgotten Man offers an interesting glimpse into one aspect of his role in the 1920s that has not often been recognized. Mencken assumed that his Forgotten Man, civilized and superior though he was, was also culturally and politically isolated, since neither his tastes nor his values prevailed. The very term "forgotten" suggested that Mencken's ideal citizen was alienated to some degree from the prevailing tendencies of American life. To suggest what reality there may have been behind this assumption, one must consider the situation in which many middle class Americans found themselves during the decade. They were normally law-abiding; but if they drank, used contraceptives, or read certain magazines or books, they were breaking the law. In so doing, they did not feel themselves to be antisocial. They still believed in individualism, honesty and hard work. They were still attracted to the verities of home and community, stability and tradition; but such values were under increasing pressure in the 1920s. Postwar changes in American society challenged these values at almost every level. F. Scott Fitzgerald indulged in a bit of romantic exaggeration when he proclaimed all gods dead and all faiths shaken. Nevertheless, the decade was a time of insidious moral crisis, as Fitzgerald and most of the best writers of the period were well aware.[9]

If, however, the Forgotten Man sought to reassert the old values, he often found them seemingly devalued. Most of the self-appointed defenders of the old virtues came from a rural and religious background that made those values seem either old-fashioned or irrelevant to more urban, sophisticated Americans. In the hands of a Bryan, a Coolidge, or a George Lorimer (editor of the *Saturday Evening Post*), middle class values appeared trite. Worse, they were often used to bolster such dubious issues as Fundamentalism and Prohibition or to hammer home demands for political and cultural conformity. Mencken's Forgotten Man still believed in the old verities, but found it difficult to express them without sounding like the

preachers, the superpatriots, and the politicians from whom he re-
coiled.

Mencken appeared to provide a solution. By positing these values
as the code of an aristocracy of character—the "civilized
minority"—Mencken enabled both the Forgotten Man and himself
to cling to a traditional value structure that could be made to seem
superior and even advanced. This assumption was, of course, un-
warranted: and, by claiming that democracy was somehow antagonistic to these values, Mencken added to the confusion of the
period. Nevertheless, he did defend attitudes very basic to traditional middle class thought.

Snobbery was one of the more unfortunate elements involved in
Mencken's ministrations to the Forgotten Man, to whom he offered
the mantle of the "civilized minority." That mantle had once been
reserved for those whose superiority had been based on esthetics
and not status. Yet, even this snobbish aspect of Mencken's appeal is
not quite so frivolous or irresponsible as it seems. Status, never very
clear-cut in America, had been blurred by the new economic habits
of the postwar era; for new modes of consumption were challenging
the more traditional methods of defining and identifying social position. Even property was no longer a satisfactory sign of status, at
least not for the growing number of white collar workers. Theirs was
a new middle class whose aspirations for status went beyond their
modest opportunities for obtaining property. Since membership in
Mencken's "civilized minority" was self-selective (what reader
would have classified himself under the suborder *homo boobiens?*),
Mencken offered some easy assurances to the Forgotten Man about
his instrinsic worth and place in the society. This affectation was the
defiant gesture of those covertly alienated from the culture of boob-
ery and Babbittry.

The political implications of Mencken's appeal to the Forgotten
Man are harder to pin down but are nonetheless suggestive. In
previous periods of American history, middle class discontent and
frustration had sometimes found outlets in movements such as
Abolitionism and Progressivism. But what sort of reform movement
could have been mounted against the dullness and mediocrity that
characterized so much of American politics in the decade? In
Mencken's first editorial in the *Mercury*, he pictured the Forgotten
Man faced with an irrelevant choice between a Progressivism that
no longer seemed credible and a form of conservatism that was

narrow, mean, and self-serving. Although Mencken pomised nothing more than solace for those caught in this dilemma, he was, in
fact, groping toward some new political response. He was urged on
in this pursuit by no less a figure than his friend Senator James Reed
of Missouri. Wishing Mencken luck with his new magazine, the
*Mercury,* Reed was confident that Mencken would succeed "because what is needed is a man who does not fly off at a tan-
gent . . . neither committing himself to new fancies of reform or
[so] anchoring himself to the rock of conservatism that he is incapable of movement. We are living in an age of transition. The thing
today is to develop a philosophy which will meet new conditions
without doing violence to old and sound principles."[10]

This search for a new political stance based on "old and sound
principles" is exactly what Mencken himself intended, as can be
seen in his letter to Nathan (quoted in Chapter 6) where he claimed
that the *Mercury* could provide leadership for the enlightened
minority. Mencken even entertained a vague hope that some sort of
third party movement would emerge out of the vacuum. In the early
1920s he had urged the *Sunpapers* to run an editorial calling for the
formation of a new party.[11] In *Notes On Democracy* he wrote: "For
what democracy needs most of all is a party that will separate the
good that is in it theoretically from the evils that beset it practically,
and then try to erect that good into a workable system. What it
needs beyond everything is a party of liberty" (205–206). Since
Mencken's party of libertarianism never appeared, he had to con-
tent himself with his support of such heroes of the moment as La
Follette and Al Smith.

During the decade, Mencken used the terms "civilized minority"
and "Forgotten Man" almost interchangeably. They symbolized,
however, two rather different sides of Mencken's nature. The concept of the civilized minority came out of his earlier enthusiasm for
art and iconoclasm when Mencken had hoped that a talented cultural elite could transform society. The Forgotten Man was the
product of Mencken's more defensive postwar mood when he felt
the need to locate his elite in some sort of social and even political
level.[12] Unfortunately, Mencken's political and social ideas were too
vague to produce anything more than a justification of the Forgotten
Man in his covert alienation and an invitation for him to elect himself to the elite.

By fusing the two images of the civilized minority and the Forgot-

ten Man, Mencken failed to see that he had altered his position as a
satirist and had abandoned the aggressive figure of the artist-
iconoclast. His Forgotten Man was a defensive image, more victim
than hero, more threatened than threatening. Although his satire
was as vigorous as ever and although his public image was as irre-
sponsibly brash as before, Mencken's main role in the 1920s was that
of the conserver. His headlong assaults on presidents and Pro-
hibitionists were, in effect, sallies from behind the walls where he
and the Forgotten Man were defending a vision of American life that
was passing into a disturbing and uncharted future.

CHAPTER 9

# The Libertarian

## I  In Defense of Liberty

ALTHOUGH politics for Mencken was a battle ground of personalities and values rather than of systems or institutions, he did have a rudimentary political philosophy that provided power and meaning to his social criticism and the real unity to his career. Writing to his German publisher in 1923, Mencken explained himself: "My literary theory, like my politics, is based chiefly upon one idea, to whit, the idea of freedom. I am, in brief, a libertarian of the most extreme variety, and can imagine no human right that is half as valuable as the simple right to pursue the truth at discretion and utter it when found."[1]

What made Mencken's love of liberty refreshingly free from the clichés and hypocrisy in which it is all too often embalmed by American political rhetoric was the rigorous logic with which he pursued it. "By liberty I mean the utmost freedom possible under an orderly society," he explained in his "Autobiographical Notes" in 1925 (165). This idea was sometimes difficult for even his friends to comprehend. When Mencken was asked in 1931 by the black journal, the Pittsburgh *Courier*, to support a campaign against the popular "Amos an' Andy" radio program because of its racist nature, Mencken expressed sympathy but could not go along with the protest. He told George Schuyler, a black writer, that ". . . all such crusades seem to me ill-advised and dangerous. . . . I am unalterably opposed to all efforts to put down free speech, whatever the excuse."[2] To Benjamin de Casseres he wrote in 1935, "I insist that if we had free speech [,] argument against free speech should be permitted also, for it is part of my doctrine that free speech itself may be an error. I don't believe it is, but neither do I think my conviction should choke off any man who disagrees." De Casseres

123

apparently balked at this attitude, for a few days later Mencken angrily responded, "You talk foolishness. If I am in favor of free speech I should be in favor of it up to the last limit of endurance. Thus, I argue that even those who are against it ought to be heard. It is you who make the compromise, not I."[3] Writing to an acquaintance in 1941, Mencken explained: "After all, a man who believes sincerely that Jews are a menace to the United States ought to be allowed to say so. The fact that he is wrong has got nothing whatsoever to do with it. The right to free speech involves inevitably the right to talk nonsense. I am much disturbed by the effort of the New York Jews to put down criticism. It seems to me that they are only driving it underground, and so making it more violent."[4] The legend of Mencken's anti-Semitism stems from his extreme and, perhaps, unrealistic application of his libertarianism to that problem.

Fortunately, Mencken's efforts were chiefly on behalf of individuals whose rights had been denied them. As late as 1924, he was still the only well-known American writer listed by the Sacco and Vanzetti Defense Committee as having registered a protest with them over the nature of the Anarchists' trial. Although he wrote often about the celebrated case, his interest was based entirely on the principle of the right to fair trial; for, according to one of his biographers, he believed the two men to be guilty.[5] Mencken was more personally involved with the Mooney-Billings case, which concerned two radical labor leaders who had been convicted in 1916 for a bombing conspiracy by a highly prejudiced California court and on very questionable evidence. In October 24, 1921, Mencken wrote in the *Sun* that although most people agreed that Mooney was innocent, yet he remained in prison, his real "crime" being his radicalism. Perhaps, Mencken mused, if the country had more free speech and fairer trials, it would have fewer bombs. In 1928, he wrote to the imprisoned Mooney, "It is an almost inconceivable outrage that you should be still confined in San Quentin, with the evidence of your innocence known to almost everyone." Mencken frequently lent his name to protests on Mooney's behalf, and in 1932 he wrote a letter to California Governor James Rolph, Jr., appealing for the radical's release. According to a letter to Mencken from the Mooney Defense Committee in 1931, "Tom instructs [us] to say that if he were making up a list of all his loyal friends, the name of H. L. Mencken would be high upon the roster."[6]

Mencken also sought to focus attention on the Carlo Tresca case in the 1920s. Tresca was the proprietor of a small, radical, anti-Fascist New York paper called *Il Martello*. The paper offended Mussolini's ambassador to the United States, and eventually the American government suppressed it and arrested Tresca for allegedly publishing birth control advertisements. Tresca, an alien, was convicted and was then offered the choice of being deported back to Italy or of being jailed. He wisely chose the latter. Mencken corresponded with Elizabeth Gurley Flynn, the famous "Rebel Girl," asking her for material about the case and soliciting an article from her on Tresca for the *Mercury*. In his own account of the case in the *Sun* on January 12, 1925, Mencken stormed, "What becomes of the old notion that the United States is a free country, that it is a refuge for the oppressed of other lands . . . ?" Roger Baldwin of the American Civil Liberties Union told Mencken that his was the best statement about Tresca that he had seen.[7]

Not all of Mencken's efforts on behalf of the rights of others were conducted in public. During the 1920s, Mencken struck up a correspondence with Emma Goldman, an Anarchist writer who had been deported following the Red Scare. He took articles from her for the *Mercury*, and in 1930 wrote to the Justice Department to urge it to return papers belonging to her that had been seized in a raid on the office of *Mother Earth* in 1917. He also urged the Bureau of Immigration to allow her to return to America to visit her relatives. In both cases, the responses were negative. "Bless your heart," Goldman wrote to Mencken, "how naive you are to think that you could help to change the law in my direction. It is splendid of you to want to attempt it. . . . The fact that you have tried has done me a world of good."[8] In 1940 he sent the Emma Goldman Recovery Committee a check for twenty-five dollars. His checkbook often followed his principles as he contributed to various organizations that defended political prisoners and combatted censorship.

Mencken's involvement on behalf of individuals like Mooney, Tresca, and Goldman should be seen in its proper light. Protest campaigns serve many functions. They not only organize people's genuine sympathy but are also important in holding political movements together and in disseminating propaganda. Mencken belonged to no political organizations, and he invariably had little sympathy for liberal or radical propaganda or goals. He was motivated purely on the grounds of principle and humanitarianism. In 1940, when he passed on to Thurmond Arnold a note received from a man claiming to have been wrongfully imprisoned, Mencken told Arnold that he did not have any idea about the merits of the case, "But when a man behind the bars asks for help it is hard to resist him."[9]

In the 1920s, Mencken's libertarianism was aimed largely at conservative opinion. With radicalism weak and on the defensive and with liberalism in a state of transition, momentary alliances with the left on specific issues presented no difficulties for him; but he never confused their aims with his own. He was convinced that liberals did not really believe in free speech, for he felt they would not oppose the suppression of illiberal attitudes. "I believe that I am more liberal than they are," he wrote of the liberals in his "Autobiographical Notes" in 1925. "I am against Socialism in all its forms, but I have always done all I could to help the Socialists when their rights were denied them" (169).

In the 1930s, liberalism was transformed into the image of the New Deal, and Communism, although far from popular, appeared for a time to exert a certain amount of influence among writers and intellectuals. Mencken became increasingly disturbed by this revival of radicalism. When John Dos Passos wrote in 1947 to ask Mencken to be part of a committee being organized to defend Edmund Wilson's *Memoirs of Hecate County* against the censors, Mencken complained that the Communists would invariably take over the protest. It was better for authors to fight their own battles. Nevertheless, he joined the committee.[10]

It was not just Mencken's own capitalistic bias that caused him to be disturbed by the leftward shift within the ranks of the intellectuals and writers. He was a libertarian by principle rather than by ideology. He therefore suspected and resented what he considered the hypocritical stand by left-wing ideologues who supported Stalinism in Russia and demanded free speech for Communists in America. In 1938, when Mencken wrote an article for the October issue of the *Mercury*, he accused some of the top officials in the American Civil Liberties Union of maintaining such a dual standard. For a time, a law suit was threatened. Arthur Garfield Hayes, an American Civil Liberties Union lawyer and an acquaintance of Mencken's, complained to him that his article amounted to a rejection of Communists simply for their political beliefs. Mencken certainly did not like Communism, but, as a long-time supporter of the American Civil Liberties Union, he was chiefly concerned that the appearance of Communists in the organization's leadership would weaken its usefulness.[11] Yet, although he was obviously rejecting the philosophy of the Popular Front, Mencken was not repudiating his libertarianism: he was not denying the right of people to be Communists. Less flexible than he had been in the past, he was, nevertheless, simply following the logic of his own views. Liberty, for him, was an end in itself, and commitment to it had to be absolute.

## II *The Passing of an Era and an Editor*

The December 1933, issue of the *American Mercury* was the last one to be published under Mencken's name. Ten years after he had founded the magazine, he had resigned as its editor for various personal reasons. After having edited magazines for thirty years, the fifty three year old Mencken was getting tired of the pressures and the constant trips to New York. Moreover, he was now much more involved in his domestic life; for, in 1930, he finally relinquished his position as one of America's most famous bachelors by marrying Sara Haardt from Alabama. When he married her, Mencken knew that Sara was suffering from an incurable form of tuberculosis. She was in the hospital during half of their married life; and, when her inevitable death came in 1935, Mencken was emotionally crushed.

There were, of course, other less personal factors behind Mencken's decision to leave the *Mercury*. The magazine had been losing readers since it had reached its peak of popularity in 1927. By 1929, the number of readers was down to 67,420, almost 10,000 below the 1927 figure, and the drop in circulation continued.[12] The decline of the *Mercury* was but one reflection of a gradual weakening of Mencken's popularity. The *Prejudices* series had ended with the sixth book in 1927, as there was no longer enough interest to continue it. By the following year, both the quantity and the quality of critical comment about Mencken had also perceptively declined; for intellectuals, bored with what they considered Mencken's obsessions with Methodists and Prohibition, and with his failure to cultivate new ground, regarded him as a spent force. While many of their criticisms were valid, few critics tried to understand or appreciate what Mencken had been trying to say. Only a few observers, such as Lippmann, Wilson, and Joseph Wood Krutch, had seen the serious intent beneath Mencken's now repetitious satire.

The fault, of course, was largely Mencken's. He had so successfully exploited the situation that the early 1920s had presented to his satiric abilities that he had failed to develop as the decade continued. He assumed, apparently, that the political vacuum of 1924 would, like the prosperity, last forever. Moreover, having imaginatively, if not always accurately, interpreted the forces at work in the decade, he had failed to reconsider his own judgments. The rigidity in his views, the reiteration of set themes, and the satiric pretense of uninvolvement, all of which had helped to make him popular, now began to work against him. Vincent Starrett, an early admirer, summarized the problem in 1927: "What he has been saying is stock in trade—it is expected, looked for. . . . He must continue as he began. . . . He cannot go back; he dare not now go ahead. To do either would be to cease to be Mr. Mencken, an institution."[13]

Some evidence exists that suggests that, by the end of the decade, Mencken was aware of his declining popularity and was seeking to solidify his hold on what he considered his essential, "serious" audience. He put great effort into two books in which he sought to make a realistic appraisal of religion and ethics. *Treatise on the Gods* and *Treatise on Right and Wrong* were issued in 1930 and 1934, respectively. Although he considered the former his best work, its sales were disappointing. By that time, the crash of the stock market and the Depression had brought a rude end to the Mencken era. In fact, the Great Depression exposed the serious weakness of Mencken's social criticism. Mencken's satire had worked, during the 1920s, because the decade had been full of ambiguities due to the collapse of Progressivism and the emergence of unfamiliar economic and social forces. Mencken, who had exploited such ambiguities with gusto, had peopled the political landscape with heroes and villains; but he had also imposed some pattern on the otherwise confusing events of the decade. He had continually depicted the sensitive, talented, honest, free spirits of America as engaged in an unequal combat against a society of ignorant, timorous conformists who had been constantly misled and swindled by their political, religious, and financial masters.

The Depression presented a dramatically different atmosphere; for complicated as the underlying economic problems were, the plight facing millions of Americans was certainly not ambiguous. Its every day effect on their lives was all too clear. Although the Depression brought politics back into the foreground of American life, the situation was too complex an event to lend itself to

Mencken's kind of demonology; and the cataclysm was far too massive to allow his pose of disinterestedness to retain its satiric cutting edge. Finally, the financial collapse posed a stark threat to Mencken's economic conservatism. He had been willing to belabor the excesses of capitalism when it seemed impregnable; but when the capitalistic system appeared to totter, he rallied to its support. In the 1920s, his defense of values had been covert; but his defense of capitalism, limited government, and individual self-reliance in the 1930s was overt. The days of his iconoclasm had passed.

The early years of the Depression had robbed Mencken of his old issues and had presented him with one that he was totally unable to handle. Consequently, he tried to ignore the situation, hoping, as did so many Americans, that it would go away. It was not until 1932 that he tried to deal with the Depression editorially in the *Mercury* and then only to admit an almost pathetic impotence. In January 1932, in a column entitled "What's Going On in the World," Mencken wrote that he had once believed that democracy was endurable because it supported capitalism. The politicians had followed the bankers, but the bankers now were calling upon the politicians for help. "No wonder I am upset! All my natural prejudices have been outraged. Temperamentally incapable of Socialism, . . . I find myself hanging upon a precarious branch, trying unhappily to figure out what is going to happen next" (6).

Although Mencken was soon echoing the Hooverian line of belt-tightening and predicting imminent recovery, the editor of the *American Mercury* clearly had nothing more to offer. As the readers began to turn away, Mencken tried to find ways to revamp the magazine and to halt its decline. Changes in the magazine's cover and alterations in its format—the tell-tale signs of sickness in the magazine trade—were about all he could accomplish. Growing clashes of personality and ideology that developed between him and his assistant editor, Charles Angoff, plunged the *Mercury* into additional confusion. By the time he left the magazine in December 1933, Mencken and the *Mercury* had declined together.

### III *In the Days of Roosevelt, II*

Mencken retired from the *Mercury*, but not from the American scene. He published several books during the 1930s, revised and extended *The American Language*, and wrote widely for magazines. He continued his weekly articles for the *Sun;* and, as a member of

the *Sunpapers* board of directors, he helped shape its editorial policy. Naturally, he continued to cover the presidential nominating
conventions. His correspondence remained as voluminous as ever;
and, although there were fewer literary figures among his acquain-
tances now, there were more politicians and public figures, even a
few New Dealers. He exchanged letters with Congressman
Emanuel Sellers on a proposed antilynching law, with Maury
Maverick of Texas on a law to enforce the Bill of Rights, with Justice
Felix Frankfurter on the rights of privacy (the justice in turn cited
Mencken on journalistic ethics in one of his opinions), and with
Thurmond Arnold on everything from language to the New Deal.

It was Franklin Roosevelt's New Deal which, by giving Mencken
a target, helped pull him out of his own personal depression of the
early and mid-1930s. Following his own dictum to "throw the reign-
ing rascles out," he voted for Roosevelt (and an end to Prohibition)
in 1932. As the new Deal began to assume its protean shapes, he
fired, almost by reflex action, broadsides at the burgeoning
bureaucracy and at the "wizards" of the Brain Trust. However,
Franklin Roosevelt seems to have confused Mencken for a time. He
was unnerved by the powers that the new president assumed; but,
as late as January 2, 1934, he could tell his readers in the *Sun* that
Roosevelt was "shrewd, candid and bold." He also felt that the
president was at least a "gentleman" and that, as such, "He will fight
longer, and he can be trusted farther."

On the whole, however, Mencken was already a consistent critic
of the New Deal. In the halcyon days of 1934, before the political
lines against Roosevelt had hardened, Mencken enjoyed a rather
unique position as one of the few senior, well-known journalists who
were opposed to the administration. Therefore, in December of that
year, when the time came for the annual Gridiron Banquet, where
journalists and the administration confront each other over cocktails
and gibes, Mencken was asked to give the after dinner speech.
Although his remarks were barbed, they were in keeping with the
evening's high jinks. "In the early days of the New Deal I used to do
a great deal of worrying about the Constitution. . . . But the other
day I had a postcard from a judge saying that the Constitution was
really very well taken care of. He said it was in the National
Museum here in Washington, stuffed with excelsior, and waiting for
Judgement Day. No doubt there are many Republicans there too,
but what they are waiting for I don't know."

Then came the president's opportunity to reply to the evening's good-humored critique of his administration. To everyone's surprise and initial shock, the usually urbane Roosevelt immediately launched into a vitriolic attack on the press; he called journalists lackies of the plutocrats and generally ignorant and uncultured imbeciles. Gradually, shock gave way to laughter as the assembled pressmen recognized that Franklin Roosevelt was quoting from Mencken's essay, "Journalism in America," from *Prejudices: Sixth Series*. Only Mencken was not amused. According to one biographer, he began scribbling notes for a furious rebutal. As soon as the president was finished, however, he was wheeled out; but he paused to shake hands with his outmaneuvered adversary. Mencken's own account of the evening displays only a hint of anger. He felt the president had employed a "fair device, and he carried it off very well. Despite his wide smile and insistence that I was a friend, it was plain enough that he had a grudge and was trying to get revenge. He has had plenty of grounds for wanting to do so, and he will have even more grounds hereafter."[14] For Mencken now roasted King Roosevelt, II, and his New Deal court in the *Sun* and in magazine pieces. In the *Sun* offices, Mencken helped swing the editorials into the anti–New Deal camp and worked hard to offset the influence of some of the younger "radicals" on the staff. In February 1938, when he took over as interim editor of the *Evening Sun* for three months, he tried to inject some of his old gusto into the staid paper by turning the editorial page into an anti–New Deal circus. One editorial was nothing but a mass of Ben Day dots, each one representing one of the million or so federal officeholders. Symbolically, the dots showed up badly, and the page appeared blank.[15]

Liberals and even radicals, who had known Mencken in the 1920s as a libertarian and sharp critic of New Era capitalism, were shocked by what appeared to be a sellout to conservatism. One correspondent in the Communist *New Masses* in 1936 had to remind the readers that there had been a time when "You couldn't throw a stone into a Communist Party mass meeting without hitting someone who, one time in the past, heartily agreed with Mr. Mencken's bitter assault on everything that was typically bourgeois."[16] The problem was, however, that Mencken had *not* changed; his libertarianism, built upon the solid foundations of Social Darwinism and a nineteenth century liberal's dedication to laissez faire, had never been aimed at capitalism itself. And although he heaved many a dead cat into the sanctums of Americanism, he never threw one at the Constitution, which he fretted over with an almost Federalist concern. The man who could accuse the Republican administrations of Harding, Coolidge, and Hoover of having increased the power of the state and who could conjure up, as he did in *Notes On Democracy*, the horror of the welfare state in 1926, was not likely to view the New Deal with a modicum of equanimity.

Mencken's opposition to Roosevelt and his program had been summed up in an article in the *Sun* in March 13, 1933, shortly after the president's inauguration. The country, he noted, had had two dictatorships in the past—those of Lincoln and Wilson. It now seemed about to embark on a third. Roosevelt had, so far, carried out his dictatorship with restraint. "But it is always well, when anything of the sort is set up in a presumably free country, to scrutinize it very carefully and even biliously, lest it get out of hand." Concluding, he commented, "If the American people really tire of democracy and want to make a trial of Fascism, I shall be the last person to object. But if that is their mood, then they had better proceed toward their aim by changing the Constitution and not by forgetting it. And they had better remember that Fascism means not only rough usage for crooked bankers but also rough usage for multitudes of far better men."

Mencken soon decided the specter of radicalism, rather than that of Fascism, haunted Washington; but his libertarianism remained unchanged. In the end, it at least kept him from joining the most hysterical of the hues and cries raised against the New Deal. In 1936, when playwright Channing Pollock invited him to join the American Liberty League, Mencken expressed sympathy with the concerns of the league but refused to join.[17] Although by now a respected member of Baltimore's conservative business community, Mencken's libertarianism remained a sharp contrast to the repressive tendencies that have often accompanied what passes for conservatism in America. He continued to defend free speech by attacking loyalty oaths for teachers and by dismissing Congressman Martin Dies and his Un-American Activities Committee as "goons." He testified before a Senate committee in favor of an antilynching bill, and the last article he wrote in 1948 ridiculed the racial segregation of Baltimore's sporting facilities.[18] This aspect of Mencken moved Thurmond Arnold to invite him to present the conservative position in a seminar that he was conducting at Yale University along with George Soule of the *New Republic*. Arnold assured Mencken that he was the "only person in the country who can fill the bill because, although your conclusions are different, you have the same point of view."[19]

It is not Mencken's hostility to the New Deal that may disappoint the reader today—given his philosophy, it was natural and inevitable—but his failure to make his satire hit home. There was certainly much to satirize about the New Deal, for Roosevelt often pursued conflicting and sometimes incompatible policies simultaneously. A satirist on the left could have been damaging. But Mencken's brand of economic conservatism was so hopelessly out of date, his adherence to laissez-faire principles so negative, that what could have been a biting critique often degenerated into an impotent, angry roar.

Mencken had his admirers, and he had the *Sunpapers* with him (especially after 1936), but only on domestic affairs. On international questions, the *Sun* retained a Wilsonian point of view. Following the European crisis of 1939, the paper began to support Roosevelt's foreign policy. Foreign affairs had never been Mencken's strong point. In his early days as a young journalist, he had displayed an almost Kiplingesque type of chauvinism. This attitude reemerged in the 1920s and especially in the 1930s in the form of very intense Anglophobia and isolationism. His views on Germany were hopelessly confused; for although Mencken disliked Fascism and Hitler, the bitterness of his own experience during World War I still rankled. At the same time, he retained an old, sentimental attachment to Germany that even the horrors of Hitler's anti-Semitism (exaggerated, thought Mencken) could not shake.

Moreover, Mencken was so convinced that democracy was on its way out that he professed to see little intrinsic difference between what he called the New Deal in Berlin and the New Deal in Washington. Liberty was doomed. Writing to a friend in 1940, he predicted that "the New Dealers will try to put down free speech under cover of the war and that we'll probably be a long while regaining it, if, indeed, we'll ever do."[20] His vision of the future was basically grim, no matter which way the war went. Early in 1941, he wrote to Albert G. Keller, an old associate of William Graham Sumner, that if Roosevelt was successful in taking America into the war, "the country will have on its hands the policing of the whole civilized world. It will have to maintain enormous armies, not only in Europe but also in Asia. . . ."[21] Having severed his connections with the *Sunpapers* in January of that year, Mencken withdrew into Hollins Street. An aging man, he was plagued by fears of declining health; he was nursing the memory of his dead wife; and he was disappointed and disgusted with the violent drift of events.

## IV  *Sunset and Darkness*

Yet Mencken retained an uncanny ability to shift his interests and seek new audiences. In his semiretirement, he continued his work on *The American Language* and then began a series of boyhood reminiscences. He had started writing these pieces for the *New Yorker* in 1939; and, during the early 1940s, he published three volumes of sketches of his youth, of his early newspaper days, and of some of his later experiences in the 1920s. The memoirs were well received: the sharp satire was gone, the writing style was simple, the humor, genuine and pleasant. Nonetheless, the *Days of H. L. Mencken* constitute an ingenious footnote to his long battle against modern America. The pre–World War I America depicted in the first two volumes, *Happy Days* and *Newspaper Days*, was presented as a golden age of simplicity, vitality, and individualism. He avoided sentimentality, but he gave way to nostalgia as he tried to show American what had been lost.

After the war, Mencken returned to the *Sunpapers* in 1948. He covered the nominating conventions, rediscovering for a brief moment the old, zany world of the "carnival of buncome" in the Henry Wallace campaign. By this time, however, Mencken's health, so long a subject of hypochondriacal speculation, was seriously deteriorating. He had had a slight stroke in 1939, and then he began having trouble with his eyesight and his memory. Then, shortly after the election in November 1948, he suffered a severe stroke that impaired his speech and left him unable to read or write. His was a terrible, ironic end for a man who had spent a lifetime with language. Only the devotion of his bachelor brother August, with whom he had lived since his wife's death, pulled Mencken out of the suicidal despair that followed. He regained comparatively good physical health, but his career, one of the most extraordinary in American letters, had come to an end. Death finally relieved him of his fate on January 29, 1956.

# CHAPTER 10

# *Contradictions and Conclusions*

IN trying to draw some conclusions concerning Mencken and his position within American cultural history, one immediately encounters a maze of contradictions. A very American writer in both his style and choice of subjects, Mencken sometimes cultivated an almost alien, even anti-American, image of himself. Although deeply committed to a wide variety of causes, he often pretended to a total lack of involvement with his society. A self-proclaimed iconoclast, he nevertheless used his talents for idol smashing in order to defend values that, far from being Nietzschean transvaluations, were simply solid bourgeois principles that were held in good repute at the hearthside, in the countinghouse, and even in the rectory. Conservative and even reactionary in some matters, he was almost radical in others.

These contradictions were not merely the product of the writer's desire to camouflage the private man from public gaze; for they tend to increase, not decrease, as one penetrates into Mencken's private world through letters and reminiscences. The contradictions lie within Mencken's personality: he was deeply divided in many of his attitudes, and these ambiguities found expression rather than resolution in his art.

## I  *The Immense Indifference of Things*

It is significant that the writers who stirred Mencken to produce some of his best criticism were those who, in his own words, depicted the "immense indifference of things—the profound meaninglessness of life."[1] Reviewing Theodore Dreiser's *Jennie Gerhardt* in the November 1911 issue of the *Smart Set*, Mencken tried to unravel the philosophy behind the novel: "What else have Moore and Conrad and Hardy been telling us these many years? What else does all the new knowledge of a century teach us? One by one the old ready answers have been disposed of. Today the one intelligible answer to the riddle of aspiration and sacrifice is that there is no answer at all" (153).

Mencken's reaction to his own conclusion that life was an impenetrable mystery was ambiguous. Sometimes he rejoiced in it, as in this passage from *Men Versus the Man:* "Life impresses me, most of all, by its appalling complexity. It is not static but dynamic; not a being, but an eternal becoming. The constant reaction of diversified individuals upon a fluent environment produces a series of phenomena which seems to me, at times, to be beyond all ordering and ticketing" (230). Thus life in the Menckenian universe could be complex, diversified, dynamic, and, in a peculiarly special way, free. Man was bound by natural laws but free from supernatural order. There was nothing outside or beyond the discoveries of science that was guiding, shaping, and directing mankind. Life had no ontological meaning—no God, no History with its Hegelian or its Marxian capital "H."

To Mencken, this absence of ontological meaning was a kind of freedom—the freedom of man to realize his ultimate potentiality, his own human dignity. In an exchange of letters with Theodore Dreiser, Mencken defined what he considered the scientific as opposed to the religious approach to the problems of life: "The efficient man does not cry out 'Save me, O God.' On the contrary, he makes diligent efforts to save himself. But suppose he fails? . . . He accepts his fate with philosophy, buoyed up by the consciousness that he had done his best. Irreligion, in a word, teaches men how to die with dignity, just as it teaches them how to live with dignity."[2]

Ultimately, however, the meaninglessness of life was not a really benign concept for Mencken. It was the *"intolerable* meaninglessness" that fascinated and, in spite of himself, so often shocked him. Nietzsche had brought Mencken to the threshold of Existentialism, but the critic did not have the philosophical equipment to enable him to cross it. His empirical, rationalistic turn of mind, his innate demand for things to make sense, made him frequently cry out against the *non*-sense of the blind, clockwork universe in which he felt obliged to believe. Time and again his stoical pose slipped from him, as when he found the death of a promising young novelist "a fate too cruel for understanding." When Mencken's wife died, he burst out to Ellery Sedgwick in a letter, "What a cruel and idiotic world we live in!"[3]

Mencken had contradictory reactions to his concept of meaninglessness. He could bluster to Burton Rascoe that "My notion is that all the larger human problems are insoluble, and that life is quite meaningless—a spectacle without purpose or moral. I detest all efforts to read a moral into it."[4] Yet what else was he doing when he tried to illuminate the meaningless void with the light of human dignity? It was as if, having proclaimed almost with triumph the meaninglessness of the universe, Mencken then issued one protest after another against its lack of meaning. As he himself once observed, "Man is never honestly the fatalist, nor even the stoic. He fights fate, often desperately. He is forever entering bold exceptions to the rulings of the bench of gods. This fighting makes for beauty, for man tries to escape from a hopeless and intolerable world by creating a more lovely one of his own."[5]

The creation of this lovelier world was, however, an artistic and, ultimately, an emotional impulse based on a denial of reality. For this reason, Mencken believed that poetry, as he explained in *Prejudices: Third Series,* was essentially "a series of ideas, false in themselves, that offer a means of emotional and imaginative escape from the harsh realities of everyday. In brief, . . . poetry is a comforting piece of fiction set to more or less lascivious music—a slap on the back in waltz time—a grand release of longings and repressions to the tune of flutes, harps, sackbuts, psalteries and the usual strings" (151). Man's mind turned to poetry only when inflicted with "the mood of revolt against the insoluble riddle of existence . . ." (169). Not only was poetry suspect, however; the emotions themselves could never be trusted. The only path to truth lay through empirical reason. Emotional impulses, no matter how alluring, were only potential traps for the unwary. For Mencken, the head was eternally at war with the heart.

## II  *The Head Versus the Heart*

"The taste for romance," Mencken once noted, "like the taste for impropriety, is inborn in all normal human beings. . . . The day comes when we turn inevitably from Zola to Dumas, just as the day comes when we turn from Richard Strauss to Johann. . . . [A man's] head may rule his heart for a week, a month or a year—but on some fatal day or other that head of his will succumb to sorrow, weariness, alcohol, an unbalanced ration, the coo of a baby or the perfume of a women's hair, and that heart of his will go upon a debauch straight-way."[6] The dichotomy of the head and the heart lies at the very basis of Mencken's personality. For he could not conceive of the possibil-ity of integrating he intellect with the emotions, of achieving a balance between rationality and feeling.

This problem might not have been quite so acute for Mencken had he not been himself a very emotional, indeed, sentimental person. As writer Elizabeth Shepley Sergeant noted after her first conversation with Mencken in the 1920s, "I had expected to meet an artist and an epicure, but I was hardly prepared for the sentimentalist—the solid, Germanic sentimentalist. . . ."[7] Since, however, Mencken considered the emotions to be a constant threat to the intellect, he tried to protect himself from his own emotionalism by accentuating the hard, tough-minded side of his nature. The result was a duality of personality that became obvious to almost everyone who came to know him. Sara Mayfield, an intimate friend of both Mencken and his wife, has recalled that "The carapace of H. L. Mencken, the hardboiled critic, we soon discovered, had been developed as a defensive mechanism by an extremely sensitive man." Marion Bloom, who at one point was almost engaged to Mencken, once accused him of hiding his real tenderness beneath a cover of hard cruelty. As critic Burton Rascoe put it, "It is not that he [Mencken] does not feel deeply, but that his emotions are primarily sentimental and not aesthetic, and, being a sentimental fellow, he has built up a defense mechanism of gay cynicism which stands between him and a free expression of the emotions felt and recorded."[8]

Only in music did Mencken seem to have been able to resolve the tensions between head and heart. For one thing, music obviously demanded great intellect and talent. "More than any other art, perhaps," he commented in *Prejudices: Sixth Series*, "music de-mands brains. It is full of technical complexities" (167). Yet, at the same time, it has deep emotional appeal. Mencken could thus give himself over to sentiments that in another art form, might have been embarrassing. To critic Fanny Butcher, he once confessed, "I can't think of any books that I'd like to have written. . . . Words are veils. It is hard enough to put into them what one thinks; it is a sheer impossibility to put into them what one feels." He would rather, he said, have written a symphony by Brahms than a play by Ibsen: "In music a man can let himself go. In words he always remains a bit stiff and unconvincing."[9] It is significant that one of the few orgnaizations to which Mencken belonged was a music group, the Saturday Night Club, which met for years in Baltimore. Mencken played the bass line in four-handed piano arrangements for the club, an assignment that he carried out with gusto, if not always total expertise. Those weekly meetings of music and beer were an important, central part of his life. Unfortunately, his lack of formal training in music closed to Mencken's creative impulses this one art form in which the dichotomy of intellect and emotion might have disappeared: ". . . I shall die an inarticulate man," he wrote wistfully in *Happy Days*, "for my best ideas have beset me in a language I know only vaguely and speak only like a child" (198).

### III  *The Hidden Idealist*

Unable to resolve the emotional and the sentimental parts of his nature with his rationalist principles, Mencken therefore sought to protect the more vulnerable side of his personality by throwing around it a hard shell of mannerisms and attitudes. His brave embrace of the meaningless universe, his harsh attempts to repress sentimentality, his rigid insistance on the primacy of intellect, and even his tough, masculine pose were all intended to ward off, or at least alleviate, the inevitable pain that emotional involvement produced. As a result, Mencken could sometimes appear to be callous and uncaring when he was, in fact, suffering greatly. Although his wife's death was a serious blow to him, on the weekend after the funeral he insisted on standing his turn as host to the Saturday Night Club. There was no joy in the occasion for anyone, least of all Mencken, but what seems an insensitive gesture on the surface was Mencken's way of trying to close the doors against grief. He retreated within the carapace of stoic toughness in which the intolerable meaninglessness of life could be met with a resigned shrug instead of with a painful shudder.

There was more at stake, however, than seeking protection from emotional pain. Mencken was a very egotistical man who was prone to enthusiastically committing himself to both men and ideas. Such commitments, however, exposed him to the vulnerability of disappointment. Worse, if his commitment proved wrongly placed, it meant that he had been guilty of allowing his enthusiasms (and emotions) to run ahead of his rational judgment. His desire to avoid such embarrassments explains two very basic characteristics of the man: his pretense of noninvolvement and his often bitter rejection of those who disappointed him. This latter characteristic helps to explain why he reacted so harshly to Shaw when he decided that the playwright was not an iconoclast of the heroic mold. Even the failure of an ideal could result in a dramatic rejection. When his concept of art and iconoclasm failed to have its expected impact upon society, Mencken completely abandoned literary criticism.

This pattern of behavior can be clearly seen in his relationships with other writers to whom he had lent friendship and support. Many of Mencken's literary friendships experienced deep rifts when his strict codes, both personal and professional, were somehow offended. Willard Huntington Wright, James Gibbons Huneker, Theodore Dreiser, George Jean Nathan, Sinclair Lewis and F. Scott Fitzgerald all came under varying degrees of the Menckenian ban. As Dreiser himself once told him, "The truth is that you are an idealist in things literary or where character is concerned and expect men to ring centre 100 times out of 100." After reminding Mencken of some of his misjudgments in the past, Dreiser continued, "You will probably continue for years to come to bring in tin cans from the street and set them on the mantel. But in view of past flops—you might be careful—& not too hard on your idols once they are out in the street again."[10]

In a clumsy way, Dreiser had put his finger on one of the most important aspects of Mencken's character. For, despite his lifelong attempt to play the skeptic, he was an idealist in spite of himself. He was not, of course, a philosophical idealist. Platonism, Hegelianism, and Transcendentalism, in so far as he understood these philosophies, were dismissed as fruitless attempts to escape from the harsh but necessary tyranny of empiricism. Mencken was an idealist, however, in the sense of believing that life should be governed by standards of perfection rather than by convenience. That Mencken sought to hide this idealism even from himself was the result of his need to shield his ego from the pain of disappointment and the chagrin of a misjudgment. This is one of the reasons why he was attracted to iconoclasm. His original concept of the artist-iconoclast was itself highly idealistic. Yet the iconoclast's methods could conceal that idealism. Mencken could champion one writer by denouncing another; he could defend a virtue by exposing a vice. His commitment to an ideal was not lessened by these methods, but it could be hidden. The mask of satire completed the iconoclast's disguise.

## IV *The Mask of Satire*

Mencken wrote little about the art of satire. Once, however, in a *Smart Set* review in April 1918, he provided a brief glimpse into the satirist's way of looking at things. In commenting on the discrepancy in America between the professed idealism of the people and their intense business practicality, he concluded that Americans had to master two distinct sets of politics, economics, and ethics: "the one that meets his complex and elegant notion of propriety, and the one that works." Although Mencken did not actually say so, this dualism was in fact the starting point for much of his own satiric approach to American society. He exploited instinctively the disparity between what is officially approved and what is privately done.

In his study of satirists, Leonard Feinberg indicates that satire is grounded upon such dualisms: the contradiction between reality and pretense, between what is and what society piously claims ought to be. Most men, Feinberg claims, adjust themselves to such discrepancies and become largely oblivious to them. The personality of the satirist, however, makes him acutely aware of such incongruities. His talent enables him to evolve an artistic vision from this awareness. What would be a useless and immature crankiness in other men becomes, in the hands of the satirist, "a logical search for artistic material which is suitable for his particular kind of art."[11]

Mencken's sensitivity to this central dualism of life came from his own failure to resolve the various dichotomies within himself. He was eternally pulled between individualism and determinism, meaninglessness and meaning, intellect and emotion, aloofness and commitment. In a sense, satire may have been his salvation. For, as David Worcester has suggested in *The Art of Satire*, irony, one of the modes of satire, tends to offer an escape from conflicting emotional responses to life. The ironist escapes a possible paralysis of mind and spirit by focusing on the tragic-comic results of the eternal clash between the ideal and the actual. By exploiting the duality of his own vision, he maintains his own equilibrium.[12]

In Mencken's case, satire enabled him to give vent to the idealistic streak in his nature; but at the same time, he could pretend that he was ever the hard-headed, tough, self-centered egotist. In a letter to Burton Rascoe in 1920, he asserted, "Few doctrines seem to me worth fighting for. I can't understand the martyr. Far from going to the stake for a Great Truth, I wouldn't even miss a meal for it. . . . I do not write because I want to make converts. . . . I write because the business amuses me. It is the best of sports."[13]

In Feinberg's opinion, this statement is the whole story. To him the vehemence in Mencken was esthetic, not moral: "Mencken's is an aesthetic choice [of material], not a moral one, any more than the choice of colors by Van Gogh is a moral choice."[14] To take this view, however, is to fall into the error of positing a monistic concept of man. Feinberg's artistic man is no more real than the Marxist's economic man or the hagiographer's spiritualized saint. Mencken's artistic instincts doubtlessly helped to determine the *way* he handled his material. But his inclination toward satire was hardly the sole arbiter of his choice of material and his basic reaction to it. Mencken's battle for the liberation of American letters, his stand on free speech and minority rights, his defense of the values of individualism, and his tireless protest in the name of "common decency" were not the results of a purely esthetic impulse. Mencken was genuinely committed to these things.

Nor did his use of satire conflict with this commitment. As Worcester suggests, "Satire . . . is the most rhetorical of all the kind of literature. . . . It has an aim, a preconceived purpose: to instill a given set of emotions or opinions into its readers."[15] Mencken did not expect to make converts in the sense of turning a Bryanite into an agnostic or a Coolidge Republican into a libertarian. But such people did not comprise his audience: Mencken wrote for the Forgotten Man—the responsible but politically uncommitted reader who could be swung into opposition against the Red Scare, Fundamentalism, and Prohibition. Mencken's whole style—the alternation between ridicule and didacticism, humor and vehemence—was aimed at causing the reader to view a situation through Mencken's eyes.

Mencken's insistence that he was merely engaging in a game for the amusement of himself and his sophisticated readers does not really contradict the rhetorical nature of his writings. He had to pretend such noninvolvement for both personal and artistic reasons; for as already suggested, he needed to mask his own idealistic commitments. Also, in order to remain an effective satirist, he had to adopt a persona that seemed to stand back bemused and above the battle. To have failed to do so would have ruined the special effectiveness in the rhetorical appeal of his satire. For satire distorts: it does not investigate complexities but it often tries to make the complex appear simple. The satirist is not initiating a dialogue in hopes of discovering the truth; he already has the truth (at least a point of view), and seeks to propagandize his version of it. Mencken avoided the complexities about Prohibition because he was convinced that it was a useless and dangerous social abberation. His aim was to present it in as ridiculous and unappealing a light as possible in order to cut through the complexities and win readers to his side.

According to Worcester, the satirist, "secretly aims at exposing a discrepancy in the strongest possible light. Once he has exposed it, the fewer words the better, for his insistance on pointing the moral will rob the reader of his share in the game. So long as he abstains from sermonizing, he has the reader with him."[16] The problem was that Mencken's real feelings often broke through the humor of an essay with an almost Swiftian passion. At the end of such passages, it was vitally necessary for him to pull back and to disclaim any real interest or involvement in the subject under discussion. In fact, the discrepancy between Mencken's supposed aloofness and his genuine outrage which thundered through so many of his essays was sometimes so great that only total mastery of his style kept his satiric persona intact.

One of the major ingredients for the success of this persona was Mencken's ability to personalize the values upon which his satire was based. Since most humor is founded upon fixed moral standards and values, the average humorist derives his comedy from the contrast between the actual behavior of society and the agreed upon standards that that behavior may sometimes violate. Satisfied in catching society in the act of tripping over its own ideals, he does not need to question the validity of those ideals or the wisdom of society in giving lip service to them. The satirist, however, may go one step farther. He may intrude his own moral vision, or he may at least make it *appear* that the moral standard he is using is his own. The bite of his satire comes, then, not merely from the contrast between what society says and what it does, but from the demolition of *both* society's practices *and* its pretenses. In such a case, the satirist does not wish to pose as society's inner conscience but as its exterior accuser. By so doing, he makes the satiric absurdity of a situation lie in the implication that society cannot act correctly or intelligently because its very ideals and motives are corrupted.

Mencken went out of his way to appear to criticize American society on the basis of the supposedly private values of the iconoclast, the aristocrat, or the Forgotten Man. In actual fact, these values were for the most part the common stock of middle class America. Had Mencken made this fact clear, however, the moralistic jeremiad rumbling beneath the surface of his satire would have been exposed. The disguise would have fallen away, and Mencken would have appeared in his true light: the spokesman for the old, bourgeois, individualistic America that was passing away before the pressures of the twentieth century.

## V  *The American Mencken*

Satire, then, was the very natural, almost inevitable, artistic form for Mencken. It was perfectly adapted to meeting those twin needs of his divided mind: commitment and protective aloofness. As a disguise, it fooled no one so successfully as the mummer himself. One consequence of this self-deception was that Mencken was never fully aware of the complexity of the relationship between himself and his country. As suggested earlier, Mencken dealt with two conflicting images of America: that of the visable land of follies—Babbittland—and that of an internalized vision of an America to which he was secretly but deeply attached. By taking the drastic step of making the word "American" stand for follies, he seriously diminished his ability to identify openly with the latter. The values that he preached were thus made to seem private ones that were in conflict with a supposedly degraded national character.

Therefore, Mencken found it difficult to present a clear, positive image of America that could be seen as an alternative to the negative paradise of fools and knaves that he had created in his satire. In fact, the best he could do was to present fragments of the other America he loved, as when he belatedly discovered an iconoclastic tradition in American literature. He occasionally contrasted such past heroes as John Adams, Jefferson, and Lincoln with the Hardings and the Coolidges of his own day. He celebrated the supposedly vital individualism of the 1880s and 1890s, and he was fascinated with the diversity and vitality that still survived in admass America. But Mencken's knowledge of and interest in the past was too weak, and his egotistical desire to stand aloof from the sordidness of his times was too strong to allow him to follow writers like Sherwood Anderson and Sinclair Lewis into the joyous rediscovery of a more promising image of America. The alienation that had begun for Mencken as a satiric pose eventually took on a certain reality in his own mind. As he mused privately in 1941, "My grandfather made a mistake when he came to America, and I have always lived in the wrong country. . . . [It] has been generally hostile to my welfare and aspirations. I have never been aware of its government save as an agency trying to injure me, and I have never found myself in agreement with its prevailing idea."[17]

Since Mencken believed that the basis for much of his supposed alienation from America was political, one of the most consistent elements in his career was his outspoken suspicion of democracy. The fact that democracy faced a critical challenge after World War I has tempted some critics to place Mencken within the context of antidemocractic ideologies abroad and right-wing extremism at home. Mencken was not a Fascist, nor was he a part of the reactionary tendencies in literary and cultural criticism during the 1920s and 1930s. His cultural radicalism, which questioned all standards in art, remains a sharp contrast to the view of Yeats, Pound, Eliot, and Wyndham Lewis—those critics of the right who sought order in art, if not always in politics, the imposition of order amid the chaos.[18]

Even by American standards, Mencken was not a good conservative. His commitment to cultural pluralism and his libertarian demand for complete freedom of thought and speech do not fit comfortably within the American conservative tradition. As Walter Lippmann recognized in 1926, Mencken's cultural attitudes warred with his supposedly antidemocratic opinions. "If Mr. Mencken really wishes an aristocracy he will have to give up liberty as he understands it; and if he wishes liberty he will have to resign himself to hearing *homo boobiens* speak his mind." Lippmann was "amazed" that Mencken did not recognize "how fundamentally the spiritual disorder he fights against is the effect of the régime of liberty he fights for."[19] Here again, Mencken was caught up in the muddle of his inability to reconcile conflicting impulses. He did want all the positive benefits provided by an ordered society, but he was too much the rebel to accept any sort of authoritarianism that could impose such an order. He thoroughly distrusted the political power of the masses, but he required a totally free society for the emergence of the creative individual.

Moreover, Mencken's failure to sketch even the bare bones of his aristocracy throws into question the seriousness of his search for an alternative to democracy. Throughout his writings there is a continual ambivalence toward democracy. In *Notes on Democracy*, he insists that he is not maintaining that "democracy is too full of evils to be further borne. . . . All I argue is that its manifest defects, if they are ever to be got rid of at all, must be got rid of by examining them realistically . . ." (200–201). A decade later, in his introduction to a new edition of James Fenimore Cooper's *The American Democrat*, Mencken admitted that, within the "false dogma" of equality, democracy did nonetheless contain a conception of human dignity: "I incline to think that that modicum of dignity is the chief and perhaps the only gift of democracy to mankind." And although careful as always to eschew that the democratic label himself, he did quote Cooper to the effect that the true democrat, "recognizing the right of all to participate in power, . . . will proudly maintain his own independence of vulgar domination."[20]

In the end, Mencken was much closer to the tradition of the squire of Cooperstown than to that of the reactionary intellectuals of his own day. He was a critic rather than a dedicated opponent of democracy. When one remembers that he did not criticize democracy as a political theorist but as a social moralist and as a cultural liberator, his position within the American cultural tradition begins to emerge. Emerson and Thoreau, for example, were also critics of democracy; both men believed in what they called the "majority of one." And nowhere in Mencken's writings is there so thorough a repudiation of the moral authority of democracy as there is in Thoreau's essay, "On the Duty of Civil Disobedience." Although Mencken shared little else with the Transcendentalists, he too was concerned with the moral freedom of the individual to pursue his own vision of what was just and right. The esthetic counterpart of this vision, for him no less than for Emerson and Thoreau, was what Joseph Wood Krutch dubbed Mencken's "worship of excellence"—a response to the special imperative in a democratic society to create an atmosphere conducive to the emergence of intellectual and artistic expression.[21] From these two concerns have come the ever-germinating seeds of intellectual dissent in American life, and to this tradition of moral and cultural dissent Mencken ultimately belongs.

Unless one believes that any form of dissent in a democracy is a sign of Nihilism, one cannot accept Maxwell Geismar's assertion that Mencken was the villain—the spirit that denies—among the middle generation of American modernists.[22] Mencken was often mistaken in his observations and often wrong in his conclusions. The bases for his judgments were not always sound, even by his own standards; but he was, nevertheless, seriously involved with and concerned about his society. As far as his being a negative force, Lippmann concluded his 1926 essay on Mencken by claiming that "here is nothing sinister that smells of decay, but on the contrary this Holy Terror from Baltimore is splendidly and exultantly and contagiously alive. He calls you a swine, and an imbecile, and he increases your will to live."[23]

The real weakness of Mencken's position as a social critic lies in his failure to ground his value system on a genuine theoretical concept of politics and society. His aristocracy was only an abstraction that, as a mere debating point, was useful, perhaps, for underscoring some of the weaknesses of democracy but was totally unrelated to the facts of American life. And although Mencken tried to become the spokesman for the middle class, his Forgotten Man, who was little more than a cultural and moral ideal, was isolated in a landscape barren of political and social analysis.

In his attacks on the New Deal, Mencken may have repaid the middle class for his earlier cultural apostasy. When he came to write his memoirs, however, he revealed that his main concern was less with class than with the past. America in the 1880s and 1890s had been, as far as he was concerned, a good place in which to grow up. It represented the last moments of a golden age in which Mencken's individualistic value systems had seemed to flourish. In the twentieth century America had changed; and, although Geismar partially misunderstood Mencken's role in the 1920s, he was correct when he noted that ". . . it is change in America which is the true villain of the piece, and Mencken's is in many ways the most illuminating of all these chronicles of change."[24] Mencken was, in fact, one of the chief victims of change among the writers of his generation. He lived to see what William Graham Sumner had dreaded—the passing of laissez-faire society. What was left of the once confident, late nineteenth century bourgeois liberal values of individual competition and limited government had found in Mencken their most articulate literary spokesman—and their chief mourner. His reiteration of those values in the 1920s represents, in retrospect, one of his most important contributions to the cultural debates of the decade. After the Depression, however, he was no more convincing than Herbert Hoover in attempting to revitalize them. His retreat into the nostalgia of *Happy Days* (1940) and *Newspaper Days* (1941), charming as those books are, represents a tacit admission of failure—a lamentation disguised as a celebration.

Mencken never really admitted, perhaps never quite realized, how much his nostalgia for the late nineteenth century represented his love not only for the days of his childhood but also for those aspects of life in America that he valued and fought to preserve. Much of his career actually consisted of contrasting the individualistic verities of this older America with the new, strange, and disturbing society that had emerged in the twentieth century. He was not clearly aware of this, however. For a large part of his adult life he had been like a guerrilla fighter in a country so long dominated by forces alien to him that he had forgotten that it was really *his* country he was defending. In the end, he came to believe that it was he who was an alien in America; for as he wrote in an unpublished autobiographical fragment of 1941, "Thus I have lived in the United States all my life without becoming, in any deep sense, an American."[25] Although the historian ought not judge whether or not a man should feel at one with his nation and his times, there is more than a touch of tragedy in this statement; for no man has ever been more thoroughly American than Henry Louis Mencken.

## VI  *Conclusion*

In trying to summarize Mencken's career and the role he played in the development of American culture, it is important to keep one point clearly in mind. Mencken was a journalist, as he was quite pleased to point out on various occasions. From the age of eighteen until his collapse in 1948 he wrote constantly for newspapers and magazines. This fact helps to place his literary and social criticism in perspective; for with the exception of his early works on Shaw and Nietzsche, his two books on religion and ethics, and the bulk of *The American Language*, almost everything that he published in book form was reworked from his newspaper and magazine pieces. An active journalist, always working toward daily, weekly, and monthly deadlines, Mencken had little time for contemplation. He worked fast, and he had such a total command of his style that the surviving original typescripts of his writings usually reveal few revisions or corrections.

Mencken's was a highly personal type of journalism, and during the 1920s many young newspaper men tried, at one time or another, to follow in his footsteps. Usually, they succeeded only in producing poor imitations of the famous style. Yet, it is possible that Mencken did have some impact upon the development of contemporary American journalism. Mencken's own journalistic roots lay with the journalist-critics and newspaper satirists of the *fin de siècle* period. It seems possible that he took these earlier forms of personal journalism and refashioned them so as to meet the tastes and needs of post–World War I America. The I. F. Stones, Art Buchwalds, and Russell Bakers of today are working in a journalistic tradition that if it did not originate entirely with Mencken, has certainly been shaped by him.

In the field of magazine editing, which he practiced for twenty years, there have been various claims made on behalf of his innovative impact. In 1926, Leon Whipple credited Mencken's *American Mercury* with what he called, ". . . the revolution on Quality Street where the serious magazines live. . . ."[26] Certainly, serious magazines did undergo some significant changes around the time the *Mercury* first appeared in 1924. It is not clear, however, to what extent other magazines copied Mencken's lead, and to what extent Mencken was simply among the first editors to successfully respond to the demands of a new age in magazine journalism. Take, for example, Harold Ross's *New Yorker* magazine, established in 1925. Charles Angoff, Mencken's assistant on the *Mercury*, claimed that the biographical "profiles" that the *New Yorker* made famous, were actually "born in the office of the *Mercury*."[27] One might also add that the kind of highly personal type of editing that Ross imposed on the *New Yorker* had been Mencken's stock in trade since he and Nathan had taken over the *Smart Set* in 1914. Nevertheless, it is very hard to determine just how conscious Ross and the other magazine editors of the 1920s were of Mencken's specific innovations. Only his beloved "Americana" department seems to have had a clear and long-lasting impact. Mencken actually began "Americana" in the *Smart Set* and carried it over to the *Mercury*. Since then, similar material has appeared as fillers in the *New Yorker*, in the "This England" column of Britains's *Week-End Review*, and, more recently, in the illustrated "No Comment" department of *Ms.* magazine.

Mencken's famous style was, of course, intimately connected with his life in journalism. It was designed to catch the attention of the reader and to hold it from beginning to end. His brand of satire still stands out as unique, for it does not quite seem to fit into the mainstream of American satiric writing of this century. In its boisterous, rough, and often aggressive good humor, it has closer affinities with Mark Twain and with the turn of the century vaudeville stage than with the urbane, sophisticated, and witty styles of Mencken's contemporaries, such as Franklin Pierce Adams, Dorothy Parker, Alexander Woollcott, and James Thurber. Mencken's pieces still read well, however, in spite of the fact that so many of his subjects (and victims) have passed into history. There are several reasons why Mencken's essays still have life in them. First of all, he had a fine sense of humor that often transcended the topics with which he dealt. Moreover, he had an impressive command and feeling for the American language, in its vernacular as well as in its formal modes. Finally, beneath the flash and sparkle of the satire, there is a sound syntactical structure. Mencken was the master of a clear, simple, and at times almost elegant prose style. In an age in which the jargon of the bureaucrat, the military man, the scientist, and the academician have all but clogged the spontaneous flow of American speech and writing; and even when the slang of the streets seems inarticulate and opaque, Mencken's essays still impart a vitality combined with clarity that is refreshing. Certainly, Mencken may be regarded as one of the most original stylists of American nonfiction prose in this century.

Over the years a minimal consensus concerning Mencken's role as a literary critic has emerged. Even his detractors have generally conceded that his assault upon the Genteel Tradition did help smooth the path for the emergence of a modern American literature. His scathing exposure of mediocrity and his tireless war upon sentimentality, upon escapist romance, and upon hollow didacticism in literature were necessary and certainly helpful to a rising generation of American writers. At the same time, Mencken was more than a cultural demolition expert. Most commentators have also acknowledged the value of his championing of those writers, the young and the not so young, who wanted to view America through ungenteel eyes and to describe it with an ungenteel voice. At this point, howevar, the consensus begins to break down.

Like many critics, Mencken missed the mark about as often as he hit it. He was certainly correct when he recognized the talents of writers like Dreiser, Fitzgerald, Lewis, Willa Cather, and Ring Lardner. The literary reputations of other favorites, however, such as James Branch Cabell and Joseph Hergescheimer, have been seriously eroded with the passage of time. Moreover, while he was on reasonably solid ground when he dealt with Realism and Naturalism, Mencken was generally unable to appreciate anything that was too avant garde. He published excerpts from James Joyce's *Dubliners* at a time when Joyce could have been mistaken for an Irish amalgamation of Henrik Ibsen and Thomas Hardy. When Joyce began a revolution in prose with his book *Ulysses*, however, Mencken could not comprehend the book's importance or muster much sympathy for those Americans who sought to follow the Irishman's lead. Mencken was limited even in the realm of Realism. While he could appreciate the work of a Dreiser or a Lewis, he was largely unmoved by the finer subtleties of a Hemingway. In poetry, Mencken's competence ran only to the more traditional forms and styles. His admiration for the works of Sara Teasdale or Lizette Woodworth Reese was certainly not misplaced. Yet, he remained largely unmoved by the work of practically all of those men and women now regarded as the major American poets of his day.

Clearly, Mencken's literary horizons were limited mainly to those writers who represented the twentieth century flowering of the major literary trends of the late nineteenth century. He was generally unable to follow those writers who tried to go beyond this mainstream of Naturalism and Realism. It is, nevertheless, important to recognize that Mencken's critical faults are more striking in the 1920s than in the earlier decades. In fact, by the middle of the 1920s he had ceased to be a literary critic. No doubt part of his disillusionment with art stemmed from the abandonment by some of the younger American authors of the type of literature that he had worked so hard to establish. At any rate, it is unfair to judge Mencken's standing as a literary critic solely by work produced in a period when his interest in fiction was declining.

A more important consideration than the appropriateness with which he delivered bouquets and barbs concerns the keeness of the critical tools that Mencken brought to his work. A factor in a critic's reputation is the quality of his mind, and it is upon this question that Mencken's limitations loom most formidably. He had read extensively in the Anglo-American literature of the nineteenth and early twentieth centuries and had made some impressive forays into the literature of Northern and Central Europe. Yet, Mencken seems to have been largely innocent of the works of the great critical theorists of the last century, especially those of the German and French schools. And although his mind roved widely, it did not delve down deep. He did not develop his intellect into that finely honed instrument that one might expect a great critic to possess. As a consequence, he made no original contributions to the theory of criticism. Indeed, in a century in which criticism has become increasingly academic, so often concerned with technique, form, and symbolism, Mencken hardly even seems to qualify as a literary critic. Here again, of course, it is important to judge Mencken within the context of his career and his times. The "New Criticism," which eventually came to all but dominate American universities and journals, was still in its infancy when Mencken was losing his interest in literature. With the exceptions of a few writers, such as Pound, Eliot, and, perhaps, Paul Elmer More, few of Mencken's American contemporaries can survive the scrutiny of present-day academic criticism.

Although such observations mitigate, they do not totally counter the arguments of those who would withhold from Mencken the laurels of a literary critic. Is there any clear, positive case that can be made in his favor? On one very important level Mencken did successfully fulfill at least one of the criteria for the literary critic. He bridged the gap between the writer and his public, bringing into fruitful contact ideas and people. Admittedly, a rather blurred line separates this sort of critic from the skillful popularizer, who passes on to the public a simplified (and often falsified) version of the new and the complex. Mencken certainly crossed that line at times. He was a popularizer when he undertook to explain Nietzsche and Shaw to American readers. Generally, however, he was something much better and more important. When he had a strong sympathy for a writer, as he did, for example, in the case of Dreiser, Mencken helped to create an audience for that writer that was expectant, receptive, and comprehending.

Mencken, then, occupied neither the high ground of formal criticism, nor the low ground of the consistent popularizer, but the very important middle ground where new ideas and new writers are introduced to an understanding audience that is prepared to receive them. Without such critics of the middle ground it would have been difficult for a modern American literature to have emerged. Mencken probably did more than any other single critic in the ten or fifteen years following 1908 to bring the new writers into contact with their public. He also helped these writers to a productive awareness of each other, and he helped to guide them toward new themes and new material. Finally, during this important period of cultural transition, Mencken was able to interpret for the public the meaning of the literary battles that were being waged. His views were not always correct, but he was able to get people interested in cultural questions.

As Mencken himself suggested, there is one theme that ran through almost everything he wrote: libertarianism. It is this libertarian strain of thought that most strongly binds Mencken the literary critic to Mencken the social critic, for he strove for freedom of cultural expression with the same dedicated passion that he brought to his demand for political liberty. Nevertheless, it must be admitted that Mencken's image as a literary critic is rather different from the one he projects as a social critic. Culturally, Mencken appears as a rebel. His desire for cultural liberation sent him out to topple the established literary traditions of pre-World War I America. When he applied that same instinct for liberty to his country's social and political problems, however, he appears to be less of a rebel and more of a defender or conserver of values. The problem is further complicated by the fact that Mencken's libertarianism will not fit comfortably into the molds of either American liberal or conservative thought in this century. Thus, while he may seem liberal on cultural matters, he often appears conservative on economic questions. Basically, of course, Mencken belonged to neither the liberal nor the conservative modes of thought as Americans have normally defined them. He lacked the liberal's confidence in human nature and the ability of government to ameliorate life's problems. At the same time, he rejected the conservative's commitment to cultural homogeneity. Moreover, the extreme antiauthoritarianism that Mencken developed after World War I was quite unsuitable to either side.

Although libertarianism is possibly more prevalent in America today than it was in Mencken's time, it has never emerged as a coherent and articulate third ideological force in America politics, as Mencken had once hoped it would. It remains a political instinct, an emotional response that while powerful at times, has never been able to establish an independent direction of its own. Perhaps the idea of a movement of individualists is a contradiction in terms; for libertarianism may represent a form of individualism so extreme that it almost precludes any conception of society coherent enough to bear the weight of an ideology. Thus, in his worst moments Mencken depicted society as nothing more than a Darwinian arena in which the individual was locked in grim combat with his competitors. In his best moments, however, Mencken had a much wider vision. His insistence that a society should treat its citizens with honor and with dignity was quite simple, quite unoriginal, and yet, quite stirring. In a century that has seen the violation of human beings carried out with bureaucratic efficiency and scientific precision, this moral basis of Mencken's social criticism cannot be simply shrugged aside. In every society in every age there must be men and women who will raise their voices in the cause of justice and human dignity. This Mencken did, often and with eloquence.

# Notes and References

## Chapter One

1. "On Living in Baltimore," *Prejudices: Fifth Series* (New York, 1926), pp. 240–41.

2. "Good Old Baltimore," *Smart Set* (May 1913), p. 113.

3. For an excellent account of Mencken's *literary* relationship with the South, see Fred C. Hobson, Jr., *Serpent in Eden. H. L. Mencken and the South* (Chapel Hill, 1974).

4. For an interpretation that places much greater stress on Mencken's German and Southern background, see D. C. Stenerson, *H. L. Mencken: Iconoclast from Baltimore* (Chicago, 1971), pp. 47–56.

5. Letter from Mencken to A. G. Keller, December 15, 1939, New York Public Library.

6. Mencken, "Autobiographical Notes: 1925," p. 73, Enoch Pratt Free Library, Baltimore, Maryland.

7. As early as 1905, Mencken wrote in the Baltimore *Morning Herald* of November 29: "He [Mark Twain] is the premier American humorist, but he is also the premier American novelist." Clipping, Mencken Room, Enoch Pratt Free Library, Baltimore.

8. Quoted in Carl Bode, *Mencken* (Carbondale, 1969), p. 23.

9. Quoted in Larzer Ziff, *The American 1890s: The Life and Times of a Lost Generation* (London, 1967), p. 150.

10. See Mencken's comments in his essay on Ade in *Prejudices: First Series* (New York, 1919), pp. 121–22.

11. Richard Bridgeman, *The Colloquial Style in America* (New York, 1966), p. 136.

12. Henry F. May, *The End of American Innocence: A Study of the First Years of Our Own Time, 1912–1917* (New York, 1959), pp. 201–02.

## Chapter Two

1. See Mencken's comments reprinted in *H. L. M. The Mencken Bibliography*, compiled by Betty Adler with the assistance of Jane Wilhelm (Baltimore, 1961), p. 46. Hereinafter, Adler.

2. Alan S. Downer, *Fifty Years of American Drama, 1900–1950* (Chicago, 1957), p. 39.

3. Not only does Mencken's humor reflect the broad parodies of the burlesque stage, but he frequently referred to specific features of the old burlesque shows in his writing, such as: "slapstick," "bladder," and "Krausmeyer's Alley."

4. "Mere Opinion," Baltimore *Herald*, December 24, 1905.

5. "The Last Round," Baltimore *Evening Sun*, April 6, 1911.

6. "The Literary Olio," *Smart Set* (February 1909), p. 155.

7. "George Bernard Shaw as 'A Hero,'" *Smart Set* (January 1910), p. 154.

8. All quotations are from the 1913 edition, unless otherwise noted.

9. Quoted in Frederick J. Hoffman, *The Twenties: American Writing in the Postwar Decade* (New York, 1955), p. 304.

10. For a brief but excellent discussion of Nietzsche's influence in prewar America, see May, pp. 206–10.

11. Guy Jean Forgue has suggested that the movement from Darwin and Spencer to Nietzsche was natural for Mencken because of certain affiliations between Darwinism and the German's philosophy. This view is no doubt correct, although Nietzsche expressly decried the influence of Darwin's teachings. However, I would reject the implication that Nietzsche was already "Darwinized" when Mencken read him. As Forgue himself points out, the mechanistic Materialism in Mencken's American form of Social Darwinism warred with the central core of Nietzsche's Exestentialism. See Forgue's *H. L. Mencken, L'Homme, l'Oeuvre, l'Influence* (Monaco, 1967), p. 92.

12. Writing in the 1930s to A. G. Keller (who had succeeded to Sumner's chair at Yale), Mencken commented, "The books of your old chief, Dr. Sumner, made a powerful impression on me when I was young, and their influence has survived." The letter, dated January 5, 1932, is reprinted in Guy Jean Forgue, ed., *The Letters of H. L. Mencken* (New York, 1961), p. 337. For the influence of Sumner on Mencken, see Stenerson, pp. 21–30.

13. R. R. LaMonte and H. L. Mencken, *Men Versus the Man, A Correspondence Between Rives La Monte, Socialist, and H. L. Mencken, Individualist* (New York, 1910), p. 25.

14. *Ibid.* pp. 119–20, 205.

15. Quoted in George Allen Morgan, *What Nietzsche Means* (Cambridge, Massachusetts; 1941), p. 212.

16. "The Prophet of the Superman," *Smart Set* (August 1913), p. 154. Forgue rightly points out that Mencken had trouble connecting his scientism, with its assumption that truth could be empirically established, to Nietzsche's more instinctive and passionate intuition of truth. However, Forgue goes too far in suggesting that Mencken forces on Nietzsche a form

of bourgeois utility of the kind epitimized by Henry Ford. See Forgue, *Mencken*, p. 97.

17. See Richard Hofstadter, *Social Darwinism in American Thought, 1860–1915* (Boston, 1955), pp. 104, 110, 202; Eric F. Goldman, *Rendezvous with Destiny, A History of Modern American Reform* (New York, 1960), pp. 73–76.

18. Stenerson, pp. 117–18.

19. May, p. 209.

## Chapter Three

1. For the history of the *Smart Set*, see Carl R. Dolmetsch, *The SMART SET: A History and Anthology* (New York, 1966); Andy Logan, *The Man Who Robbed the Robber Barons* (London, 1966); Frank Luther Mott, *The History of the American Magazines, Vol. V: Sketches of 21 Magazines, 1905–1930* (Cambridge, Massachusetts; 1968).

2. Quoted in Howard Mumford Jones, *The Theory of American Literature* (Ithaca, 1965), p. 122.

3. Quoted in Grant C. Knight, *The Strenuous Age in American Literature* (Chapel Hill, 1954), p. 127.

4. All dates in parentheses in this chapter refer to the *Smart Set* unless otherwise noted in the text.

5. Quoted in Richard Ruland, *The Rediscovery of American Literature: Premises of Critical Taste, 1900–1940* (Cambridge, Massachusetts; 1967), p. vii.

6. Quoted in William H. Nolte, ed., *H. L. Mencken's SMART SET Criticism* (Ithaca, 1968), p. 25.

7. "A Novel of the First Rank," *Smart Set* (November 1911), p. 153. At least one writer agreed with Mencken's idea about the alien quality of good writing in America. Willa Cather, after reading his essay, "Our National Letters," wrote to Mencken in February 6, 1922: "I've often had a deep inner tooth ache of the soul, wondering whether I was unconsciously copying some 'foreign' writer. When Oh Pioneers was written, it was a terribly lonesome book; I couldn't find any other that left out our usual story machinery. I wondered then . . . whether my mind had got a kink put in it by the four shorter novels by Tolstoi. . . . I used to wonder if they had so 'marked' me that I could not see the American scene as it looked to other Americans. . . ." Mencken Collection, New York Public Library.

8. "The Folk Song," Baltimore (Sunday) *Sun*, 1909, bound in "Editorials and Dramatic Reviews, Baltimore Sun 1906–1910," p. 127, Mencken Room, Enoch Pratt Free Library.

9. "On American Stage Plays," Baltimore *Evening Sun*, bound in "Editorials and Other Articles, Baltimore *Sun*, 1910–1912," p. 227, Mencken Room, Enoch Pratt Free Library.

10. Quoted in Nolte, *Smart Set*, (Howells) pp. 6, 178; (James) p. 13.

11. *Ibid.*, p. 274.

12. "The Vernal Bards," Baltimore *Evening Sun*, April 14, 1911.

13. "Introduction," *We Moderns: Enigmas and Guesses*, by Edwin Muir (New York, 1920), pp. 14, 15.

14. *A Bathtub Hoax and Other Blasts & Bravos From the CHICAGO TRIBUNE*, ed., Robert McHugh (New York, 1958), p. 109.

15. For a well-balanced evaluation of Mencken's comments on Poetry, see Carl R. Dolmetsch, "H. L. Mencken as a Critic of Poetry," *Jahrbuch für Amerikastudien*, XIX (Heidelberg, 1966), pp. 83–95.

16. I recognize the difference between what Spingarn called, coining the phrase, "The New Criticism" and the variety of academic approaches to literature that are, perhaps erroneously, still included in that term.

17. Quoted in Donald M. Hensley, *Burton Rascoe*, Twayne United States Authors Series (New York, 1970), p. 71.

### Chapter Four

1. Quoted in Adler, p. 49

2. *Ibid.*

3. Untitled and unsigned editiorial in Baltimore *Sun*, dated 1911, Mencken Room, Enoch Pratt Free Library.

4. "Roosevelt in Europe," bound in "Editorials and Other Articles, Baltimore *Evening Sun*, 1910–1912, VI, 14, Mencken Room, Enoch Pratt Free Library.

5. Unless otherwise noted, all dates enclosed in parentheses in this chapter, except in Section III, refer to "Free Lance" articles printed in the Baltimore *Evening Sun*.

6. Baltimore *Sun*, 1911, pencil dated clipping, Mencken Room, Enoch Pratt Free Library.

7. For an interesting argument against the concept of a Progressive movement, see Peter G. Filene, "An Obituary for 'The Progressive Movement,'" *American Quarterly* XXII (Spring 1970), pp. 20–34.

8. For Mencken's claim to have voted for Roosevelt, see "The Last Gasp," Baltimore *Evening Sun*, November 1, 1920.

9. Clyde Griffen, "The Progressive Ethos," in *The Development of an American Culture*, eds. Stanley Coben and Lorman Ratner (Englewood Cliffs, New Jersey; 1970), p. 130.

10. See Mencken's "Preface" and the chapter entitled "Munich" in *Europe After 8:15* by Mencken, George Jean Nathan, and Willard Huntington Wright (New York, 1914).

11. "The American" (June 1913), pp. 87–94; "The American: His Morals" (July 1913), pp. 83–91; "The American: His Language" (August 1913), pp. 89–96; "The American: His Ideas of Beauty" (September 1913), pp. 91–98; "The American: His Freedom" (October 1913), pp. 81–88; "The American: His New Puritanism" (February 1914), pp. 87–94. All articles are in the *Smart Set*. All dates in Section III of this chapter refer to this series.

12. Quoted in May, p. 365.

13. Mencken to E. Sedgwick, September 1, [1914], Forgue, *Letters*, p. 49.

14. Mencken to E. Sedgwick, December 29, [1915], *ibid.*, p. 76.

15. Mencken to F. H. Garrison, August 30, 1918, *ibid.*, p. 128.

### Chapter Five

1. See Robert E. Spiller et al, *Literary History of the United States*, rev. ed. (New York, 1953), pp. 1135–56, 1358–60.

2. May, pp. 219–329; 333–34.

3. Walter Lippmann, *Drift and Mastery: An Attempt to Diagnose the Current Unrest* (New York, 1914), p. xviii.

4. See Ernest Earnest, *The Single Vision: The Alienation of American Intellectuals* (New York, 1970), pp. 3–21.

5. For a detailed discussion of Humanism and Mencken's controversy with the Humanists, see Chapters One through Four of Ruland.

6. For the key role that Dreiser's reputation played in the literary debates of this period, see May, pp. 189–91, 389–91.

7. For Mencken's attitude toward Sherman, see his letter to Carl Van Doran, September 1, 1936, Forgue, *Letters*, p. 408.

8. Stuart Pratt Sherman, *Americans* (New York, 1922), p. 11.

9. Mencken to P. Marks, February 23, [1923], Forgue, *Letters*, p. 244.

10. Stuart Pratt Sherman, *The Genius of America* (New York, 1923), p. 28.

11. The statement is from the introduction to Mencken's unpublished anthology of short stories, "Modern American Short Stories" (1921), p. 6. The typescript is bound and is part of the Mencken Collection at the Enoch Pratt Free Library.

12. "My Dear Walpole. An Open Letter from H. L. Mencken," *Bookman* (December 1925), pp. 438–39. For Walpole's letter see the November 1925 issue of the same journal, pp. 246–48. For an earlier exchange of open letters between the two men see the *Bookman* (May 1922), pp. 255–58; (June 1922), p. 364.

13. In his book *Americans*, Stuart Pratt Sherman condemned *The American Language* as "designed as a wedge to split asunder the two great English-speaking peoples. . . ." p. 10.

14. In 1963, Raven I. McDavid, Jr., brought out in one volume a revised version of the fourth edition of *The American Language* and the two supplements.

15. Stenerson, p. 219.

16. Stuart Pratt Sherman, *Critical Woodcuts* (New York, 1926), p. 242.

### Chapter Six

1. For the history of the *Smart Set* and Mencken's involvement with the magazine, see (in addition to works cited in footnote one of Chapter 3): Carl

R. Dolmetsch, "A History of the *Smart Set* Magazine, 1914–1923" (doctoral dissertation, University of Chicago, 1957); Burton Rascoe and Groff Conklin, eds., *The SMART SET Anthology* (New York, 1934).

2. Many of Mencken's biographers tend to see Wright as little more than Mencken's protégé. Rascoe and Conklin depict Wrights' editorship of the *Smart Set* as the high point in the magazine's history and denegrate the later efforts of Mencken and Nathan. Dolmetsch gives a balanced view of the merits of all parties involved.

3. Mencken to T. Dreiser, April 29, [1915], Forgue, *Letters*, p. 70.

4. Mencken to T. Dreiser, December 16, 1916, *Letters of Theodore Dreiser*, vol. I, ed. Robert Elias (Philadelphia, 1959), p. 239.

5. Quoted in Sara Mayfield, *The Constant Circle: H. L. Mencken and His Friends* (New York, 1968), p. 167.

6. Dolmetsch, "A History of the *Smart Set* Magazine," p. 121.

7. May, p. 215.

8. Ruland, p. 116.

9. T. Dreiser to Mencken, April 26, 1915, Forgue, *Letters*, p. 69. For Pound's comment, see Pound to Mencken, September 27, 1916, *The Letters of Ezra Pound 1907–1941*, ed. D. D. Paige (New York, 1950), p. 98.

10. Randolph Bourne, "H. L. Mencken," in *War and the Intellectuals: Collected Essays, 1915–1919*, ed. Carl Resek (New York, 1964), p. 164.

11. *Ibid.*

12. Pound to Mencken, January 1919, *The Letters of Ezra Pound*, p. 146.

13. See, for example, Mencken to E. Boyd, March 13, [1919], Forgue, *Letters*, p. 142.

14. For "aesthete" reactions to Boyd's article and the publishing of *Aesthete: 1925* (a copy of which is in the library of the University of Pennsylvania) see Malcolm Cowley, *Exile's Return: A Literary Odyssey of the 1920's* (New York, 1951), pp. 190–93; Matthew Josephson, *Life Among the Surrealists: A Memoir* (New York, 1962), pp. 267–69, 289–91; M. K. Singleton, *H. L. Mencken and the AMERICAN MERCURY Adventure* (Durham, North Carolina; 1962), pp. 49–52.

15. Mark Schorer, *Sinclair Lewis: An American Life* (New York, 1961), pp. 290–91; William F. Goldhurst, *F. Scott Fitzgerald and His Contemporaries* (Cleveland and New York, 1961), p. 90.

16. Henry Dan Piper, *F. Scott Fitzgerald: A Critical Portrait* (London, 1966), p. 130.

17. Mencken to Burton Rascoe [Summer 1920?], Forgue, *Letters*, pp. 189–90; Mencken to L. Untermeyer, November 25, [1920], *ibid.* p. 211.

18. "The Ulster Polonius," *Smart Set* (August 1916), 140; reprinted in *Prejudices: First Series*, pp. 181–90.

19. "Ibsen, Journeyman Dramatist," *Dial* (October 11, 1917), p. 323; see also "More Notes on Books—2," *Smart Set* (November 1921), p. 141.

20. Mencken, review of *The Nietzsche-Wagner Correpsondence*, *Atlantic Monthly* (February 1922), p. 14.

21. See Edgar Kemler, *The Irreverent Mr. Mencken* (Boston, 1950), pp. 114–16; Stanley Weintraub, "Apostate Apostle: H. L. Mencken as Shavophile and Shavophobe," *Educational Theater Journal*, XII (October 1960), 184–90.

22. *James Branch Cabell* (New York, 1928), p. 12.

23. *Prejudices: Third Series* (New York, 1922), p. 93.

24. H. G. Wells, *The New Machiavelli* (New York, 1910), pp. 23, 24.

25. Singleton, p. 33.

26. Mencken to U. Sinclair, August 24, [1923], Forgue, *Letters*, pp. 258–59.

27. Quoted in Singleton, p. 56.

28. Mencken to G. J. Nathan, October 19, [1924], Forgue, *Letters*, pp. 268–70.

## Chapter Seven

1. Mencken to E. Wilson, May 26, 1921, Forgue, *Letters*, p. 225. See Edmund Wilson's article, "H. L. Mencken," *New Republic*, XXVII (June 1, 1921), pp. 10–13.

2. The *Tribune* series ran until 1928. The McHugh collection, *The Bathtub Hoax*, reprints some of these pieces. A *Carnival of Buncombe*, ed. Malcolm Moos (Baltimore, 1956) is a collection of Mencken's articles on politics, written for the *Sunpapers* from 1920 until 1938.

3. All dates in this chapter refer to articles in the Baltimore *Evening Sun*, unless otherwise noted.

4. "Americanism: Exterior View," *Smart Set* (April 1923), p. 140.

5. The banning of the *Mercury* and the subsequent trial, better known as the "Hatrack Case," is discussed in all the Mencken biographies and in Singleton, pp. 167–81. For background to Boston censorship during the 1920s, see Paul S. Boyer, "Boston Book Censorship in the Twenties," *American Quarterly*, XV (Spring 1963), 3–24.

6. Richard Hofstadter, *The Age of Reform* (New York, 1960), p. 289.

7. See James H. Timberlake, *Prohibition and the Progressive Movement* (Cambridge, Massachusetts; 1963); Kenneth K. Baily, *Southern White Protestantism in the Twentieth Century* (Gloucester, New York; 1968).

8. I therefore feel that Anthony Channell Hilfer confuses the issue when he includes Mencken among his "Village Rebels" in his study, *The Revolt from the Village, 1915–1930* (Chapel Hill, North Carolina; 1969).

9. See William R. Manchester, *Disturber of the Peace. The Life of H. L. Mencken* (New York, 1950), p. 140; Kemler, p. 185; Bode, p. 265; and Mencken to E. L. Masters, May 27, 1925, Firestone Library, Princeton University. For Mencken's articles on the trial and reminiscences by some

of the participants in the trial, see *D-Day at Dayton, Reflections of the Scopes Trial*, ed. Jerry R. Tompkins (Baton Rouge, Louisiana; 1965).

10. See Paul Carter, *The Twenties in America* (New York, 1967), p. 83.

11. "Maryland: Apex of Normalcy," *Nation* (May 3, 1922), pp. 518, 519.

12. T. C. Cochran and William Miller, *The Age of Enterprise: A Social History of Industrial America* (New York, 1961), p. 324.

13. *Ibid.*, p. 332.

14. Hofstadter, p. 287.

15. Goldman, p. 245.

16. For a study of Mencken's editorship of the *Mercury*, see Singleton.

17. Hoffman, pp. 313, 314.

18. Anon., "Editorial Notes," *American Mercury* (December 1927), xcii–xciii.

19. See Singleton for the names of the better-known contributors to the *Mercury*.

20. [Mencken] "Preface," *Three Years, 1924–1927. The Story of a New Idea and its Successful Adaptation* (New York, 1927), unsigned.

### Chapter Eight

1. Mencken to J. Tully, August 20, 1936, Firestone Library, Princeton University.

2. Mencken also lent his talents to further the presidential ambitions of two personal friends, Senator James Reed of Missouri and Governor Albert Ritchie of Maryland.

3. "Autobiographical Notes: 1941," loose sheet, Enoch Pratt Free Library.

4. Anders Iversen, "Democratic Man, The Superior Man and the Forgotten Man in H. L. Mencken's *Notes On Democracy*," *English Studies*, L (1969), 354.

5. "Young Bob," Baltimore *Evening Sun*, August 3, 1925.

6. "Al in the Free State," Baltimore *Evening Sun*, October 29, 1928. Mencken's enthusiasm for Smith may have been largely for public consumption. Among the Mencken-Smith letters in the New York Public Library, there is a note by Mencken to the effect that early on in the campaign he realized that Smith would make an "incredibly bad President." This note is not dated and might have been the product of protective hindsight. If it did reflect Mencken's opinions at the time, however, it suggests that he consciously tried to make Smith into a hero and a symbol. Perhaps, like those journalists who lionized Charles Lindbergh, Mencken was intuitively aware of the decade's need for heroes.

7. Mencken to F. Butcher, February 20, [1921], Forgue, *Letters*, p. 219. Writing to novelist Percy Marks on December 2, [1922], Mencken promised that he would write "the book I have had in mind for a long while,

to wit, 'Advice to Young Men,' a frank, realistic, unsentimental treatise . . . revolving around the doctrine that the most precious possession of man is *honor*" (239). Although he did gather notes for such a book, it was never written.

8. D. C. Stenerson, "The 'Forgotten Man' of H. L. Mencken," *American Quarterly* XVIII (Winter 1966), 687.

9. See Irving Howe's essay, "American Moderns," in *Paths of American Thought*, eds. Arthur Schlesinger, Jr., and Morton M. White (London, 1954), p. 314.

10. J. Reed to Mencken, September 3, 1923, New York Public Library.

11. Bode, p. 195.

12. Certainly, by the end of the decade some portion of Mencken's readership was solidly placed in the upper middle class. According to a readership survey dated May 1, 1931, 39.2 percent of the magazine's readers had an annual income of ten thousand dollars or more. Thirty-five percent of subscribers were bankers, corporation officials, or business executives. Thirty-one percent were professional men. This survey is bound in "Mercury Miscellanea" in the Mencken Room of the Pratt Library. Yet the *Mercury's* audience was not necessarily ultraconservative. In December 2, 1932, Mencken wrote to Knopf, his publisher, stating that the liberal *Nation* duplicated more of the *Mercury's* subscription list than either *Harper's* or the *Atlantic Monthly*. Forgue, *Letters*, p. 343.

### Chapter Nine

1. Mencken to Georg Müller, 1923, Mencken Room, Enoch Pratt Free Library.

2. Mencken to G. Schuyler, June 15, 1931, Forgue, *Letters*, p. 330.

3. Mencken to B. de Casseres, March 2, and March 5, 1935, Firestone Library, Princeton University.

4. Mencken to L. Birkhead, January 22, 1941, Forgue, *Letters*, p. 454.

5. Manchester, p. 177.

6. Mencken to T. Mooney, July 11, 1928; Tom Mooney Defense Committee to Mencken, July 9, 1931. Both letters in New York Public Library.

7. "The Land of the Free," January 12, 1925, Baltimore *Evening Sun*; R. Baldwin to Mencken, January 16, 1925, New York Public Library.

8. E. Goldman to Mencken, May 20, 1930, New York Public Library.

9. Mencken to T. Arnold, March 29, 1940, New York Public Library.

10. Mencken to J. Dos Passos, January 27, 1947, New York Public Library.

11. See A. G. Hayes to Mencken, April 25, 1938, New York Public Library. The American Civil Liberties Union had apparently read the article before it was to be published. Mencken did rewrite it slightly and the controversy never overflowed into court.

12. Singleton, p. 214.

13. Vincent Starett, *Haldeman-Julius Monthly* (December 1927), pp. 123–25.

14. Mencken's speech and his account of the evening are in the F. D. Roosevelt folio in the Mencken collection of the New York Public Library.

15. For Mencken's activities on the *Sun* at this time, see Bode, pp. 197–200.

16. Quoted in Daniel Aaron, *Writers on the Left: Episodes in American Literary Communism* (New York, 1961), p. 412.

17. C. Pollock to Mencken, December 27, 1935; Mencken to Pollock, January 9, 1936, New York Public Library.

18. See, *The Vintage Mencken*, ed. Alistair Cooke (New York, 1955), pp. 227–30.

19. T. Arnold to Mencken, November 18, 1937, New York Public Library.

20. Mencken to Mrs. Olga Ross, June 3, 1940, Herman Schapiro folder, Mencken Room, Enoch Pratt Free Library.

21. Mencken to A. Keller, February 17, 1941, New York Public Library.

*Chapter Ten*

1. *A Book of Prefaces* (New York, 1917), p. 11.

2. Mencken to T. Dreiser, November 3, [1909], Forgue, *Letters*, p. 9.

3. Mencken to E. Sedgwick, June 7, [1935], *ibid.*, p. 392.

4. Mencken to B. Rascoe [Summer 1920], *ibid.*, p. 188.

5. "Editorial," *American Mercury* (July 1927), p. 288.

6. "Novels—The Spring Crop," *Smart Set* (May 1911), p. 165.

7. Elizabeth Shepley Sergeant, *Fire Under the Andes* (New York, 1927), p. 241.

8. Mayfield, p. 115. Marion Bloom quoted in Bode, p. 153. Some very revealing comments on Mencken are to be found in Marion Bloom's correspondence to her sister in the Mencken Collection, New York Public Library. The Rascoe quote is from Hensley, p. 73.

9. Mencken to F. Butcher, February 20, [1921], Forgue, *Letters*, pp. 219, 220.

10. T. Dreiser to Mencken, September 23, 1920, *ibid.*, pp. 198–99.

11. Leonard Feinberg, *The Satirist: His Temperament, Motivation and Influence* (New York, 1965), p. 145.

12. David Worcester, *The Art of Satire* (New York, 1960), p. 141.

13. Mencken to Rascoe, [Summer 1920(?)]; Forgue, *Letters*, p. 188.

14. Feinberg, p. 39.

15. Worcester, p. 8.

16. *Ibid.*, p. 42.

17. "Autobiographical Notes: 1941," loose sheet, Enoch Pratt Free Library.

18. See John R. Harrison, *The Reactionaries* (London, 1967).

19. Walter Lippmann, "H. L. Mencken," *Saturday Review of Literature* III, (December 11, 1926), p. 414.

20. "Introduction" to James Fenimore Cooper's, *The American Democrat or Hints on the Social and and Civic Relations of the United States of America* (New York, 1956), pp. viii, ix.

21. Joseph Wood Krutch, "Antichrist and the Five Apostles," *Nation*, CXIII (December 21, 1921), 733–34.

22. Maxwell Geismar, *The Last of the Provincials: The American Novel, 1915–1925* (Boston, 1947), pp. 376–77.

23. Walter Lippmann, "H. L. Mencken," *Saturday Review of Literature*, III (December 11, 1926), 413.

24. Geismar, pp. 376–77.

25. "Autobiographical Notes: 1941," loose sheet, Enoch Pratt Free Library.

26. Singleton, p. 181.

27. *Ibid.*, p. 182.

# Selected Bibliography

PRIMARY SOURCES

1. Bibliography

*H. L. M. The Mencken Bibliography.* Compiled by Betty Adler with the assistance of Jane Wilhelm. Baltimore: The Johns Hopkins Press, 1961.

*Menckeniana: A Quarterly Review.* published by the Enoch Pratt Free Library, Baltimore. Since 1962 has kept the Adler bibliography up to date.

"A Descriptive List of H. L. Mencken Collections in the U.S." Compiled by Betty Adler. Baltimore: Enoch Pratt Free Library, 1967.

2. Library Collections

The Mencken Room, Enoch Pratt Free Library, Baltimore, Maryland.

The Manuscript and Archives Division of the New York Public Library, New York City.

The Library of Princeton University, Princeton, New Jersey.

The Dreiser Collection, Library of the University of Pennsylvania, Philadelphia, Pennsylvania

3. Published Correspondence

*The Letters of H. L. Mencken.* Selected and annotated by Guy J. Forgue. New York: Knopf, 1961.

*The New Mencken Letters.* Ed. Carl Bode. New York: Dial, 1977.

*Letters of Theodore Dreiser: A Selection.* 3 vols. Ed. Robert H. Elias. Philadelphia: University of Pennsylvania, 1959.

4. Major Separate Works by Mencken

*George Bernard Shaw: His Plays.* Boston: Luce, 1905.

*The Philosophy of Friedrich Nietzsche.* Boston: Luce, 1908; rev. ed., 1913.

*A Book of Prefaces.* New York: Knopf, 1917.

*In Defense of Women.* New York: Knopf, 1918.

*Prejudices: First Series.* New York: Knopf, 1919. Subsequent books in this series, all published by Knopf, are: *Second Series,* 1920; *Third Series,* 1922; *Fourth Series,* 1924; *Fifth Series,* 1926; *Sixth Series,* 1927.

*The American Language; A Preliminary Inquiry into the Development of English in the United States.* New York: Knopf, 1919. Revised editions

166

were brought out in 1921, 1923, and 1936. *Supplements I* and *II* were published in 1945 and 1948, respectively.

*Notes On Democracy.* New York: Knopf, 1926.

*James Branch Cabell.* New York: McBride, 1927.

*Treatise On the Gods.* New York: Knopf, 1930.

*Treatise On Right and Wrong.* New York: Knopf, 1934.

*Happy Days, 1880–1892.* New York: Knopf, 1940.

*Newspaper Days, 1899–1906.* New York: Knopf, 1941.

*Heathen Days, 1890–1936.* New York: Knopf, 1943.

5. Introductions and Contributions to Books

Introductions to *A Doll's House* and *Little Eyolf* by Henrick Ibsen. Boston: Luce, 1909.

*Men Versus the Man, a Correspondence between Rives La Monte, Socialist, and H. L. Mencken, Individualist.* New York: Holt, 1910.

"Munich." In H. L. Mencken, George Jean Nathan, Willard Huntington Wright, *Europe After 8:15.* New York: Lane, 1914.

"Preface." In George Jean Nathan and H. L. Mencken, *The American Credo: A Contribution toward the Interpretation of the National Mind.* New York: Knopf, 1920.

"Introduction." In Edwin Muir, *We Moderns: Enigmas and Guesses.* New York: Knopf, 1920.

"Politics." In *Civilization in the United States,* ed. Harold Stearns. New York: Harcourt, 1922.

"Introduction." In James Fenimore Cooper, *The American Democrat or Hints on the Social and Civic Relations of the United States of America.* New York: Vintage, 1956.

6. Mencken as Editor

A. Newspapers

Mencken held a variety of editorial positions on both the Baltimore *Herald* and the Baltimore *Sunpapers.* See the Adler bibliography for positions and dates.

B. Magazines

*Smart Set.* Co-editor with George Jean Nathan from 1914 until 1923.

*The American Mercury.* Co-editor with George Jean Nathan from 1924 until 1925 and then editor from 1925 to 1933.

7. Newspaper and Magazine Articles

A. General

Baltimore *Herald,* 1899 to 1906. Clippings in Enoch Pratt Free Library, Baltimore.

Baltimore *Sunpapers,* intermittently from 1906 to 1948. Two important series were:

"The Free Lance," May 8, 1911 to October 23, 1915.

"Monday Articles," February 9, 1920 to January 31, 1938.

*Smart Set.* Monthly book reviews from 1908 to 1923 plus many miscellaneous articles.

*The American Mercury.* Monthly book reviews and editorials in most issues from January 1924 to December 1933.

B. Selected Magazine Articles

"The American," *Smart Set*, XL (June 1913), 87–94. The other articles in this series, listed by subtitle, are: "His Morals," XL (July 1913), 83–91; "His Language," XL (August 1913), 89–96; "His Ideas of Beauty," XLI (September 1913), 91–98; "His Freedom," XLI (October 1913), 81–88; "His New Puritanism," XLII (February 1914), 87–94.

"Ibsen: Journeyman Dramatist," *Dial*, LXIII (October 11, 1917), 323–26.

"Literary Capital of the United States," *Nation* [London], XXVII (April 17, 1920), 90–92.

"Maryland: Apex of Normalcy," *Nation*, CXIV (May 3, 1922), 517–19.

"Fifteen Years," *Smart Set*, LXXII (December 1923), 138–44.

"What's Wrong with *The Nation?*", *Nation*, CXXVII (November 21, 1928), 542–43.

"What I Believe. Living Philosophies XII," *Forum*, LXXXIV (September 1930), 133–39.

"Ten Years," *American Mercury*, XXX (December 1933), 385–87.

"Notes On Negro Strategy," *Crisis*, XLI (October 1934), 298, 304.

8. Recorded Material

*H. L. Mencken Speaks.* Caedmon Records, TC-1082.

9. Anthologies

*A Mencken Chrestomathy.* Ed. H. L. Mencken. New York: Knopf, 1949.

*The Vintage Mencken.* Ed. Alistair Cooke. New York: Vintage, 1955.

*Prejudices, A Selection.* Ed. James T. Farrell. New York: Vintage, 1958.

*The Bathtub Hoax and Other Blasts & Bravos From the CHICAGO TRIBUNE.* Ed. Robert McHugh. New York: Knopf, 1958.

*H. L. Mencken on Politics, a Carnival of Buncombe.* Ed. Malcolm Moos. New York: Vintage, 1960.

*H. L. Mencken on Music, A Selection.* Ed. Louis Cheslock. New York: Knopf, 1961.

*H. L. Mencken, The American Scene. A Reader.* Ed. Huntington Cairns. New York: Knopf, 1965.

*D-Day at Dayton: Reflections on the Scopes Trial.* Ed. Jerry R. Tompkins. Baton Rouge: Louisiana State University, 1965. Contains Mencken's dispatches on the trial.

*H. L. Mencken's SMART SET Criticism.* Ed. William Nolte. Ithaca, New York: Cornell University, 1968.

*The Young Mencken: The Best of His Works.* Ed. Carl Bode. New York: Dial, 1973.

*The Young Mencken: The Uncollected Writings.* Ed. Carl Bode. New York: Dial, 1973.

*A Gang of Pecksniffs, and Other Comments on Newspaper Publishers, Editors and Reporters.* By H. L. Mencken. Ed. Theo Lippman, Jr. New Rochelle, New York: Arlington House, 1975.

*Mencken's Last Campaign: H. L. Mencken On The 1948 Election.* Ed.
   Joseph C. Goulden. Washington, D.C.: New Republic Books, 1976.
*Mencken Versus the Middle Class: A Collection of Mencken's "americana."*
   Ed. H. Alan Wycherley. New York: International School Book Service,
   1977

SECONDARY WORKS

1. Unpublished Doctoral Dissertations
DOLMETSCH, CARL R. "A History of the *Smart Set* Magazine, 1914–1923."
   Doctoral dissertation, University of Chicago, 1957. Indispensible for
   Mencken's role as critic and editor, with much information not con-
   tained in Dolmetsch's published *History* (see below).
STENERSON, DOUGLAS C. "A Genetic History of the Prejudices of H. L.
   Mencken, 1880–1926," Doctoral dissertation, University of Minnesota,
   1961. Emphasizes early development and continuity of Mencken's
   ideas.
THOMA, GEORGE NICHOLAS. "A Study of the Rhetoric of H. L. Mencken's
   Essays, 1917–1927." Doctoral dissertation, University of Chicago,
   1958. Includes discussion of rise and decline of critical approval of
   Mencken.
WILLIAMS, W. H. A. "H. L. Mencken. A Critical Study, 1880–1929."
   Doctoral dissertation, The Johns Hopkins University, 1971.
2. Biographies of Mencken
BODE, CARL. *Mencken.* Carbondale and Edwardsville: Southern Illinois
   University, 1969. Presents the conservative, domestic, and personal
   side of the man.
GOLDBERG, ISAAC. *The Man Mencken, a Biographical and Critical Survey.*
   New York: Simon, 1925. Impressionistic and overwritten. Makes use of
   Mencken's own autobiographical notes and reprints some youthful
   material.
KEMLER, EDGAR. *The Irreverent Mr. Mencken.* Boston: Little, Brown,
   1950. Critical and provoking portrait of the "demagogic" Mencken.
MANCHESTER, WILLIAM R. *Disturber of the Peace. The Life of H. L.
   Mencken.* New York: Harper, 1950. Readable but rather uncritical
   romp with Mencken's public personality.
3. Memoirs
ANGOFF, CHARLES. *H. L. Mencken, A Portrait from Memory.* New York:
   Yoseloff, 1956. A highly critical presentation of the vulgar Mencken.
   Quotations of conversations are interesting but "from memory." Au-
   thor never knew when Mencken was joking.
MAYFIELD, SARA. *The Constant Circle: H. L. Mencken and His Friends.*
   New York: Delacorte, 1968. Warm, informal portrait of Mencken and
   his wife by a close friend.

4. Critical Studies and Monographs

BOYD, ERNEST. *H. L. Mencken.* New York: McBride, 1925. The first and still one of the best books on Mencken from an Irish critic who knew him well.

DOLMETSCH, CARL. *The SMART SET: A History and Anthology.* New York: Dial, 1966. Most of the historical section devoted to the Mencken-Nathan years. The serious student will still want to consult the author's doctoral thesis (see above).

FORGUE, GUY JEAN. *H. L. Mencken, l'Homme, l'Oeuvre, l'Influence.* Monaco: 1967. Published doctoral thesis for the University of Paris. An important study of the sources of Mencken's ideas by the editor of the Mencken letters.

HOBSEN, JR., FRED C. *Serpent in Eden: H. L. Mencken and the South.* Chapel Hill: University of North Carolina Press, 1974. A good study of Mencken's relations with Southern writers, both as individuals and as groups.

NOLTE, WILLIAM. *H. L. Mencken. Literary Critic.* Middletown, Connecticut: Wesleyan University, 1964, 1966. The author, whose own prejudices tend to match Mencken's, presents his case enthusiastically, if somewhat uncritically. His anthology of Mencken's *Smart Set* pieces makes a more convincing argument for Mencken's critical abilities (see above).

SINGLETON, M. K. *H. L. Mencken and the AMERICAN MERCURY Adventure.* Durham, North Carolina: Duke University, 1962. Important study of Mencken's editorship of the *Mercury*.

STENERSON, DOUGLAS C. *H. L. Mencken. Iconoclast from Baltimore.* Chicago: University of Chicago, 1971. Largely devoted to the pre-1920s Mencken, this book is a sound study of the origin and development of the critic's ideas.

WAGNER, PHILIP. *H. L. Mencken.* University of Minnesota Pamphlets on American Writers, No. 62. Minneapolis: University of Minnesota, 1966. Brief introduction by a friend and colleague.

5. General Studies Containing Material on Mencken

A. The Depression and War Years. Most commentaries on Mencken in these years tended to reflect the political concerns of the writers as much or more than their views on literature.

ALLEN, FREDERICK LEWIS. *Only Yesterday, an Informal History of the Nineteen-Twenties.* New York: Harper, 1931. Journalistic in the best sense, this readable yet stimulating book set the tone for future attitudes toward Mencken and the Age of Ballyhoo.

CARGILL, OSCAR. *Intellectual America, Ideas on the March.* New York: Macmillian, 1941. Tries to fit Mencken into the context of anti-democratic European influences on modern American literature. The author later sought to make amends for his attack in his less satiric and more balanced "Mencken and the South," *Georgia Review*, XI (Winter 1952), 369–76.

GOLD MIKE. *The Hollow Men*. New York: International Publishers, 1941. Party line Marxist attack from the editor of the *New Masses*.

HICKS, GRANVILLE. *The Great Tradition, an Interpretation of American Literature since the Civil War*. New York: Macmillan, 1933. A better-balanced Marxist critique.

KAZIN, ALFRED. *On Native Ground, an Interpretation of Modern American Prose Literature*. New York: Reynal, 1942. This classic work contains one of the best informed critical evaluations of Mencken written in this period.

KRONENBERGER, LOUIS. "H. L. Mencken." In *After the Genteel Tradition*, ed. Malcolm Cowley. New York: Norton, 1937. Mencken as seen by one of the refugees of the lost generation.

RASCOE, BURTON, AND GROFF CONKLIN, eds. *The SMART SET Anthology*. New York: Reynal, 1934. Contains an anti-Mencken account of the magazine by one of his earliest champions.

B. The Postwar Years. Although some of the old attacks on Mencken are reiterated, writers and scholars in this period are generally more objective and astute in their evaluations of the critic and more interested in fitting him into his cultural context.

BEWLEY, MARIUS. *The Complex Fate: Hawthorne, Henry James, and Some Other American Writers*. New York: Grove Press, 1954. An interesting critique that suffers from the author's having taken Mencken's supposed antimoralism at face value.

BROOKS, VAN WYCK. *The Confident Years: 1885–1915*. New York: Dutton, 1952. A final summing up by an important contemporary.

GEISMAR, MAXWELL. *The Last of the Provincials, The American Novel, 1915–25*. Boston: Houghton, 1947. Contains one of the most important and stimulating postwar essays on Mencken.

GOLDMAN, ERIC F. *Rendezvous with Destiny, a History of Modern American Reform*. New York: Vintage, 1960. Contains a brief but provocative attempt to fit Mencken into 1920s liberalism.

HARTSCHORNE, THOMAS L. *The Distorted Image: Changing Conceptions of the American Character Since Turner*. Cleveland, Ohio: Case Western Reserve University, 1968. Discussion of Mencken in terms of the debate over American character during the 1920s.

HILFER, ANTHONY CHANNELL. *The Revolt from the Village, 1915–1930*. Chapel Hill: University of North Carolina, 1969. Tries to fit Mencken into the tradition of the "Village Rebels."

HOFFMAN, FREDERICK J. *The Twenties, American Writing in the Postwar Decade*. New York: Viking, 1955. Critical of Mencken's love-hate relationship with the middle class.

LEARY, LEWIS. "H. L. Mencken: Changeless Critic in Changing Times." In

*The Young Rebel in American Literature*, ed. Carl Bode. New York: Praeger, 1960. The final summation of the case of the lost generation against its rejected father figure.

MAY, HENRY F. *The End of American Innocence: A study of the First Years of Our Own Time, 1912–1917*. New York: Knopf, 1959. An excellent piece of cultural history, this book is important for helping to fit Mencken into the cultural debates of this period.

MCCORMICK, JOHN. *American Literature, 1919–1932*. London: Cape, 1960. A narrowly based, highly critical view.

RULAND, RICHARD. *The Rediscovery of American Literature. Premises of Critical Taste, 1900–1940*. Cambridge, Massachusetts: Harvard University, 1967. A most important book with a judicious discussion of Mencken's role as a critic and an evaluation of the Mencken-Sherman debates.

YATES, NORRIS W. *The American Humorist: Conscience of the Twentieth Century*. New York: Citadel, 1965. Presents an analysis of the personae in Mencken's satire.

C. Biographies and Studies of Contemporaries. Recent studies of writers with whom Mencken was at one time closely associated have thrown important light on both the man and his influence.

HENSLEY, DONALD M. *Burton Rascoe*. Twayne United States Authors Series. New York: Twayne, 1970.

GOLDHURST, WILLIAM F. *F. Scott Fitzgerald and His Contemporaries*. Cleveland and New York: McGraw, 1961.

MILLER, JAMES E. *F. Scott Fitzgerald, His Art and Technique*. New York: New York University, 1963.

PIPER, HENRY DAN. *F. Scott Fitzgerald: A Critical Portrait*. London: Bodley Head, 1966.

SCHORER, MARK. *Sinclair Lewis: An American Life*. New York: McGraw, 1961.

SCHWAB, ARNOLD. *James Gibbons Huneker: Critic of the Seven Arts*. Stanford, California: Stanford University, 1963.

SWANBERG, WILLIAM A. *Dreiser*. New York: Scribner, 1965.

6. Articles

A. Evaluations by Contemporaries. With a few exceptions, Mencken's contemporaries fell into two camps: those who concentrated on the negative side of his position as a critic, and those who, in defending him, emphasized his positive attributes. The three writers who appear at the end of this section could be called the "independents." They belonged to no "schools" of critics and their comments, usually well balanced and original, survive the partisan battles of the 1910s and the 1920s.

1. Positive

ARMSTRONG, EVERHARDT. "Mencken and America." *Nineteenth Century*, CI (January 1927), 117–25.

BOYD, ERNEST. "American Literature or Colonial?" *Freeman*, I (March 17, 1920), 13–15.

FITZGERALD, F. SCOTT. "Baltimore Anti-Christ." *Bookman*. LII (March 1921), 79–81.

RASCOE, BURTON. "Fanfare." Chicago *Sunday Tribune*, (November 11, 1917), part 8, 7. Reprinted in *H. L. Mencken: Fanfare* along with an essay by Vincent O'Sullivan. New York: Knopf, 1920.

VANDORAN, CARL. "Smartness and Light, H. L. Mencken, Gadfly for Democracy." *Century*, CV (March 1923), 791–96.

2. Negative

ANONYMOUS. "Mustard Plaster Mencken." *Bookman*, LXIV (December 1926), 388.

ANONYMOUS. "The Passing of H. L. Mencken." *Bookman*, LXX (October 1929), 186–88.

BABBITT, IRVING. "The Critic and American Life." *Forum*, LXXIX (February 1928), 161–76. Beginning of the New Humanist counterattack.

BOURNE, RANDOLPH. "H. L. Mencken." *New Republic*, XIII (November 24, 1917), 102–103. Cogent criticism by a literary radical.

BOYTON, PERCY. "American Literature and the Tart Set." *Freeman*, I (April 7, 1920), 88–89.

CANBY, H. S. "Federalist: 1925 Model." *Saturday Review of Literature*, II (December 12, 1925), 401, 409. Mencken as neo-Federalist.

CHESTERTON, G. K. "The Sceptic as Critic." *Forum*, LXXXI (February 1929), 65–69. Conservative Catholic view.

JOHNSON, GERALD W. "The Congo, Mr. Mencken" *Reviewer*, III (July 1923), 887–93. Sharp dissent from Mencken's attack on the South in "Sahara of the Bozart." Author eventually became a colleague and admirer of Mencken.

KUMMER, FEDERICK A. "Something Must Have Happened to Henry." *Bookman*, LXV (June 1927), 408–10.

RASCOE, BURTON. "Notes for an Epitaph," New York *Evening Post* (March 4, 1922). Critical reevaluation by a former admirer.

ROOT, RAOUL; JANE HEAP; AND MARGARET ANDERSON. "Three Views of H. L. Mencken." *Little Review* (January 1918), 10–14. Dissenting opinions from the avant garde.

SHERMAN, STUART PRATT. "Beautifying American Literature." *Nation*, CV (November 29, 1917), 593–94.

———. "Mr. Mencken, the Jeune Fille, and the New Spirit in Letters." *New York Times Book Review* (December 7, 1919), 718. Reprinted in the author's *Americans*. New York: Scribner, 1922.

———. "Mr. Brownell and Mr. Mencken." *Bookman*. LX (January 1925), 632–34.

SPRINGARN, JOEL E. "The Growth of the Literary Myth." *Freeman*, VII

(May 2, 1923), 181–83. A just complaint about Mencken's interpretation of the author's theory of the new criticism.

3. The Independents

KRUTCH, JOSEPH WOOD. "Antichrist and the Five Apostles." *Nation*, CXIII (December 21, 1921), 733–34.

LIPPMANN, WALTER. "Near Machiavelli." *New Republic*, XXX (May 31, 1922), 12–14.

———. "H. L. Mencken." *Saturday Review of Literature*, III (December 11, 1926), 413–14.

WILSON, EDMUND. "H. L. Mencken." *New Republic*, XXVII (June 1, 1921), 10–13.

———. "The All-Star Literary Vaudeville." *New Republic*, XLVII (June 30, 1926), 159–60.

———. "Mencken's Democratic Man." *New Republic*, XLIX (December 15, 1926), 110–11. The last two essays are reprinted in Wilson's *Shores of Light, a Literary Chronicle of the Twenties and Thirties*. New York: Farrar, 1952.

B. Recent Scholarly Articles

Since 1966, *Menckeniana* has published useful articles on various aspects of Mencken.

BLOOM, ROBERT. "Past Indefinite: The Sherman-Mencken Debate on the American Tradition." *Western Humanities Review*, XV (Winter 1961), 73–81.

COWING, CEDRIC B. "H. L. Mencken, the Case of the 'Curdled' Progressive." *Ethics*, LXIX (July 1959), 255–67. An interesting if not quite satisfactory interpretation of Mencken's early political ideas.

DOLMETSCH, CARL R. "H. L. Mencken as a Critic of Poetry." *Jahrbuch für Amerikastudien*, XIX (Heidelberg, 1966), 83–95.

FULLINWIDER, S. P. "Mencken's American Language." *Menckeniana: A Quarterly Review*, 40 (Winter 1971), 2–7.

MARTIN, E. A. "The Ordeal of H. L. Mencken." *South Atlantic Quarterly*, LXI (Summer 1962), 326–38. An interesting attempt to relate the domestic side of Mencken's life to his thought.

RUBIN, LOUIS D. "H. L. Mencken and the National Letters." *Sewanee Review*, LXXIV (Summer 1966), 723–38. A reappraisal of Mencken's role as a critic.

STENERSON, DOUGLAS C. "The 'Forgotten Man' of H. L. Mencken." *American Quarterly*, XVIII (Winter 1966), 686–96. An analysis of the ideas behind Mencken's concept of the ideal citizen.

WEINTRAUB, STANLEY. "Apostate Apostle: H. L. Mencken as Shavophile and Shavophobe." *Educational Theater Journal*, XII (October 1960), 184–90. Criticizes the reversal of Mencken's attitude toward Shaw without quite getting to the heart of the problem.

# Index

(The works of Mencken are listed under his name)

175

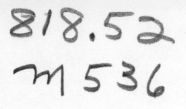